Geepe

and other writings

'Geepers, I love you'

Marie and Joe Gladden in an undated photo. Sally Gladden, their daughter, found love letters in a closet and decided to write a play based on her parents love during the Depression era. See story on page 3

Geepers, I Love You
and other writings

Sally Gladden

Copyright © 2017 by Sally Gladden.

Library of Congress Control Number: 2016916657
ISBN: Hardcover   978-1-5245-4932-9
                 Softcover   978-1-5245-4931-2
                 eBook   978-1-5245-4930-5

All rights reserved. No part of this book may be reproduced or transmitted in any form or by any means, electronic or mechanical, including photocopying, recording, or by any information storage and retrieval system, without permission in writing from the copyright owner.

This is a work of fiction. Names, characters, places and incidents either are the product of the author's imagination or are used fictitiously, and any resemblance to any actual persons, living or dead, events, or locales is entirely coincidental.

Any people depicted in stock imagery provided by Thinkstock are models, and such images are being used for illustrative purposes only.
Certain stock imagery © Thinkstock.

Print information available on the last page.

Rev. date: 02/16/2017

To order additional copies of this book, contact:
Xlibris
1-888-795-4274
www.Xlibris.com
Orders@Xlibris.com
750977

PREFACE

"Geepers, I Love You" by Sally Gladden, is an original two-act play. While rummaging through trunks in the attic of my home (205 Chapel Street, Fayetteville, NY), I found love letters that Parker Gladden (AKA Park- my DAD), a lonely Fayetteville, NY barber had written to his lady, Marie Hamilton (my MOM) , while she was away in nursing school in Brooklyn, NY. The time is 1932-33, The Great Depression, when jobs were few, haircuts were 25 cents, marathon dancers gleaned attention, and all hoped that Roosevelt would save the country.

The primary scene is Park Gladden's barber shop, Fayetteville, NY. Parker writes his long letters to Marie while he awaits customers. Unfortunately, it is "starve the barber time " for many in the village of Fayetteville. The economy is horrid for all. Parker would have preferred to be a musician but his family needed his income as a barber. He is lonely; he drinks excessively; he tries to remain humorous amidst the stresses of the time. Voice-overs of Parker reading these letters to Marie serve as segues between scenes. These letters are insightful, funny, tragic and all-telling about being the "Barber of Funnyville" during the Depression. Colorful people come to Park's barbershop and conversations give us insight about the people and the effects of the Depression on all. These customers, from the very young to old-timers,share the newspaper news, happenings of the small village, gossip and, in general, conversations about life!

A secondary scene is the nurse's station in Brooklyn,where Marie is seen reading many of Park's letters. She is also dealing with her Nurse Supervisor, Nurse Katrina (the wicked, the dictator).

In this two-act play, to while away the hours, Park listens to the radio, composes music, practices his trombone and writes letters to his "Nurtz" while he awaits customers. Prior to Act I and during the intermission, the audience sees projections of the Depression Era and hears music of that era.

The play is happy, sad, informative and the characters are real. The playwright interviewed many citizens who endured the Depression locally. The characters are based on real people.

Special thanks goes to all who encouraged me to write this book. My family was lovingly patient. I am especially thankful to Elizabeth Dopp, my niece, who is my computer wizard.

I was completely "daddy's girl" growing up. I attribute my joking, talents and inquisitiveness about life to him. Nancy, my older sister, was much like my mom. She was orderly, a great multi-tasker and serious. Unfortunately, I was too young to really recall my grands mentioned in these writings as they were deceased by the time I entered the World.

The Depression Era affected all. I was pleased to have had the opportunity to interview local people (Sullivan County, NY where I reside presently) who had been through the 1930s. Their values and lives were different from today's. I call them SURVIVORS. All were such fun to speak with as they transported me back to when they were younger.

Geepers, I LOVE YOU

an original 2 act play by Sally Gladden.

Premiered by The Sullivan County Dramatic Workshop at the Rivoli Theatre, South Fallsburg, NY, September 7-16, 2007. News article, production review and cd are available for perusal.

"Geepers" received several
awards from The Theatre Association of NY (TANYS)
Original production cast:

Parker Gladden.......Jason Hill
Sully................Mike Gastwirth
Floyd..................Sundar Pratt
Joe.....................Daniel Stein
Hottie.................Anthony Chanov
Frank..................Leonard Deduke
Marie Hamilton...........Petra Santiago
Katrina Algermissen..Heather Strauss
Teddy..................Matthew Side
Leroy...................Lawrence Myers
Pete, the Mailman.....Frank Simone
Fred Quackenbush....Albee Bockman
Edith Quackenbush.....Lucie Evans
Roberta................Jamee Bockman
Dot Hamilton...........Sommer Johansen
Grace................... Kayla Luczyski
Radio Announcer......Tom DelFavero

THE CAST: 7 M, 6 F (Flexible casting)
Parker. M, 28, AKA "PARK-The Barber of Funnyville"
Barbershop customers: (parts may be merged or omitted)
Sully... elderly man, bank manager
Lloyd... 4-5 year old boy
Joe,40
Frank, 50
Louie, any age

Teddy, 20, slow
LeRoy
Fred
(Male and female extras if needed)
Hotty/Hotdog.................... M, 26, huge, burly, crude
Marie................................ F, 25, Registered Nurse, Park's "Nurtz"
Katrina (aka Big Nurse).... F,40, German accent
Mrs. Quakenbush................ F, 40-5, "battle-axe" wife of Fred, cameo part
Robert (a)........................... young girl or boy, 13
Dot (Marie's sister)............ F, 25, snotty
Grace................................. F, 20's, pretty

TIME/PLACE: November 1932-March 1933. Fayetteville, NY. NOTE: During the lengthy voice-overs, power-point photos representative of the Depression Era are flashed on screens and/or or auditorium walls.

SET: (AREA 1) The primary set depicts a 1930's small, one chair barber shop, Fayetteville, NY. We see PARK'S BARBERSHOP written on the UC window. We see the red and white barber pole outside. Interior: Barber chair, barbering instruments, humidor, customers' chairs, various wall hangings. A large mirror dresses a counter that has drawers. Various tonic and bay rum bottles are on the counter. There is a 1930's Cathedral or Tombstone radio on the counter. There is a coat rack and various magazines in a cubby table. A brass spittoon is by the door. A photo of Marie stands on the counter. Leaning against the counter is a wooden board/plank used as a booster seat for youngsters. We see the front door and the curtained doorway to the back room.

(Area 2) DR or DL is a small stage or caliper for the nurse's station. Suggest a counter, patients' charts on wall. Lit only during the nurse station scenes.

ACT I

-1-

AT RISE: Parker unlocks the front door for the morning's routine with newspaper in hand. He pulls up the shade on the center window. It is a bright sunny morning but chilly in November. During Park's morning routine, the VOICE-OVER and music dominate. The year is 1932, Herbert Hoover, a Republican, is campaigning against FDR and his New Deal. Park turns on the radio. The radio plays "Little Orphan Annie". Park goes into the back room, rummages about, returns with a Barbasol container (for disinfecting combs); places on counter. Park changes stations to a comedy show with music. Park plugs in his clippers. He pampers the box of paper liners which he puts on the customer before he puts on the hair catching, white/blue striped cloth. He gets a straight-edge razor from a drawer and sharpens it on the strop that is attached to the chair. He looks into the mirror and directs the music with his straight- razor as his baton.

PARK:

(Talking to the mirror) You handsome devil, you! Still got it, Parker Gladden. (Combs hair, then with Italian accent) Remember, Tony- you promised Marie that you'd ease off that demon rum! Be good! You best get with it fool - or you'll lose her! Mean old Monday morning... let's get to it!! (He winks. He goes to the coat rack to get the striped muslin cloth. He fetches the broom and dust pan from the back room. He turns over the CLOSED sign on the door to read OPEN. He turns

1

on the switch for the barber pole. He gets his stationery from a drawer and sits in chair starting to write. He switches the radio to the Syracuse Symphony- Radio announcer: "Today we bring you Mozart! This was recorded this past summer. We feature the Syracuse Symphony! Enjoy!"

MUSIC.

(VOICEOVER) PARKER:

Dearest Marie- Here 'tis I... a wee bit sleepy but possibly I can think of a bit to write this morning. It was exactly 4 when I turned in this morning but I couldn't fall asleep. I snuggled under the covers... and I thought of you. Gee whiz- another Monday morning. Miss Hamilton, I drift off at night thinking of you and awaken with only YOU on my mind. Must be love, hmmmm? It was a sad parting last night and even sadder as I was left staring at that old, wicked bus taking you away. I watched you as you hopped on that nasty bus bound for Brooklyn Hospital. It's 10 o'clock now and you must have 4 more tedious hours to go. Darn, I miss you already and you haven't even arrived at your destination! I miss your "Geepers" even though I make fun of you saying that... GEEPERS... I love you! The weeks should go by fast- pray. I will do my darndest to stay on the wagon. Demon drink cannot get me as I am in love with the most wonderful lady in the world- YOU are my world! I will while away the hours- maybe sometimes acting foolishly-as I write you from "Tony's Old Barber Shop" right here in Funnyville, NY. I have been here for 1 ½ hours now and have, as yet, no customers! We sure are in the depression years- very depressing when folks have a hard time paying 25 cents for a haircut. It is "starve the barber day" for sure. After I left you, I breezed along to Fayetteville. "Dear One" (the world is waiting for the sunrise) is playing on the radio and it sure does put me in a blue mood without you. Ah, gee whiz- I'm so nutty... 'scuse please. (The mood is interrupted by Mr. Sullivan, aka, "Sully", and his young grandson.)

SULLY:

Ah, good morning, Park! It's time for little Lloyd's first man's haircut! Are you up to it?? (Note: throughout this, Lloyd verbalizes NO or shakes his head. He is just plain stubborn!)

PARK:

Hey, there you two. Say Lloyd- are you going to be a big man getting your haircut today? I was so proud of you when you got your very first haircut a while ago! (Park puts the wooden booster board on the chair arms.) How about sitting way up here? See, I have this brush that'll tickle your neck. (He lightly tickles his neck!) Here are scissors. (chop, chop). And I'll drape this cloth on you so the hair will fall on it. (Kid clings to grandpa. Both coax the kid onto the chair; the kids starts to cry and fidgets, repeating NO. NO. Sobbing)

PARK:

Say- how about if I cut your grandpa's hair first and you can help me?(Sully removes the boy from the board; Park removes board; Sully jumps into the chair. Park goes to work)

SULLY:

So Marie is off to the big city? HUH?

PARK:

That she is. Dropped her off at the Syracuse bus depot this morning. She'll study at the Brooklyn Hospital for 6 months and then she'll be qualified to be a charge nurse at Crouse-Irving... a supervisor! (He sighs) Say, son (looking down at the boy) would you help me sweep up your grandpa's hair? (Park hands him the broom and Lloyd sweeps gleefully. Park continues cutting.)

SULLY:

Good thing your dad has you to tend to the shop. Guess the old boy has to settle down a bit with that heart condition and all! I remember when I was a boy- we'd go to his shop in Manlius and Ernest would cut my hair. What a terrific sense of humor!

PARK:

That he has! Guess that's where I got my devilishness from. He still tries to be at the shop in Manlius, but he gets to coughing so hard he has to close up and goes home to rest. I worry about him trying to take on too much. This Depression is bad enough! Sure is depressing! (He coaxes the child to get on the board he puts on the arms of the chair. Child cooperates. Park talks humorously to him while draping the cloth on Lloyd.) See... it's ok. (He spins the chair!) Way up high sits the Happy Prince! Now for you, Lloyd, me boy! Say, could you help me sing that silly song about the animal fair? (Parks starts the song, kid joins in and gramps)

"I went to the animal fair;
The birds and the beasts were there.
The old baboon fell out of the moon
While combing his golden hair.
The monkey, he got drunk
He sat on the elephant's trunk.
The elephant sneezed,
And fell on his knees.
And that was the end of the monk.
the monk... the monk...

(They all laugh with "the monk, the monk. the monk". Song starts again. BLACKOUT during which they keep singing. Wig off kid. Give impression that his hair has been cut off and hair is on the floor. LIGHTS UP. Park finished cutting the kid's hair. Tickles him as he uses the brush on his neck. Puts powder on brush and douses him well. Pours witch hazel in palms and rubs the child's neck.)

SULLY:

Say, you sure do have a great way with kids, Park.

PARK:

Someday I hope to have a gaggle of kids of my own. I would love that! Realistically, Maybe two- naw- maybe a baseball team! Haw- 2... 2 seems just about right.

LLOYD:

Sing it again! Sing it again!

PARK:

You keep practicing that song!! Lost my voice (he exaggeratedly acts it out). YOU were great! (Park spins him in the chair and let's him down from the ride). The grandfather places 2 quarters in Park's hand and gives him a 10 cent tip. (Ad lib "goodbyes" as they exit. Park looks in the mirror, picks up Marie's photo and speaks…) Yeah- I sure would like to be the daddy of beautiful children with YOU… Miss Hamilton! Hope that they look like you, me Scottish lass! Mustn't have my ugly mug! (He gets his paper and pen and writes)

VOICE OVER, PARK:

Dearest Marie. Me again! (He reaches over to turn the radio which is playing doleful music.) The sad music fills my ears with grief for you! By now you are almost there! Gee whiz… here… here- I must say something to brighten my little muse! How would you like to step into a marathon dance the moment you get off the bus? After I left you- I loped along Genesee Street en route to Funnyville. I thought of that old tire blowing out. I wouldn't have minded it a bit knowing my mission was accomplished and I saw you safely on that old bus. I won't have much use for the car now that you are gone! Study hard, my girl! I'd like to take in a concert at Lowes in Syracuse tonight but I'm too poor to even think about it. Perhaps the next time we're on this earth, I'll have plenty of dough! The Conductor of the Syracuse Symphony booked me for Monday night. The gig pays $5/hour. Isn't that something? I will be a rich man! Ha! I'll try to shave Mr. Beach at his home this week and shall stop in to say hello to your mom next door! Poor guy has been house-bound for 3 weeks now.

(Enter Joe. Takes off hat and coat and hangs them up)

JOE:

Say, can you do me a fast trim? I gotta date tonight with a red hot tomato and wanna look sharp! (Joe jumps in the chair and Park does a fast trim). Thought we'd go to Minoa and check out the marathon dancers!! Three days now and they're still shuffling. By now some hoofs have to be dragging. Guess they started with 50 couples and are now down to just a few.

PARK:

Sure would be a sight! Guess the money that the winners get will hold them for a few of these wicked days. The pot is $100- big money! But ouch. my dogs would hurt!

JOE:

Would YOU do it?
(Customer enters, picks up a LIFE magazine with FDR on cover, takes seat. Ab libs, "Hello, etc.)

PARK:

I'd last a few hours maybe. Marie and I watched them as they started their dance in Syracuse last week. Couldn't even think about it. Who would mind the shop?

JOE:

Yeah, but the money...

PARK:

Yeah, the money. Let's see. At 25 cents a head. I'd need to cut 400 heads of hair for that kind of money! Maybe it's less frustrating to lower the ears of 400 customers than to drag around the dance floor for days- morning, noon and night. Guess they give them a few breaks... to use the necessary rooms and get some refreshments.

JOE:

Cripe, even when a race horse is down and done in, someone shoots him to put him out of his misery. These poor marathon dancers... by 3 days, they're dragging each other around the floor all done in! Crazy times call for crazy antics.

PARK:

Guess you need to be in good shape. No booze to slow these crazies down!

(Enter Hotty, aka "Hotdog", a car mechanic. Hotty is wild and often coaxes Park to go out drinking and drives because Park's car usually has problems.)

HOTTIE:

(Singing) Stick out your can, here comes the garbage man! (laughs heartily). Hey, all! Time to go huntin' tomorrow for a deer, but I'd rather have me a big, buxom dear (acts her out!). Say, there, tiger,- wanna knock down a few when I get back? We can start at the dance hall and who knows where from there.

PARK:

I don't know. I promised my Marie that I'd go easy and stay off the demon rum.

HOTTIE:

Now, what she don't know won't hurt her! Ya know. Hey- just a few. You need to relax some. I know where we can get some good home-made hooch... dynamite stuff! Baby, pick you up Friday at 8, and don't be late! Buh. bye.(He starts to go)

PARK:

Maybe just a few... a couple. That's it!! Two... really!!

HOTTIE:

Sure! Sure! Hey working fools need to get some relaxation. Gotta tell you about a song I just heard about our own Limestone Creek. Couple of kids was singing it at the bowling alley yesterday. They had a smelly experience! Ready?? Here goes: (overly dramatic). "He could not swim, he could not float. A big fat turd went down his throat."

PARK:

On that sick note, you're leaving! I go fishing in that creek... well, I used to. You're like a big old puppy dog- always hanging around here. (Laughter). Be gone, demon! Out, damned spot. out! (Hotty leaves laughing as Frank enters. Ad libs)

FRANK:

How's things, Hotty? Hi, Park? Not too busy today? Joe?

PARK:

That Hotty! Have to admit that's funny... darned creek is so polluted with all that sewage flowing into it... Who'd go swimming in there anymore? Used to swim in the creek in Manlius when I was a kid... who knows how polluted the waters are now? (He repeats, "I could not swim, I could not float.." Finishes the trim. Applies talc with brush on Joe's neck. He removes the cloth and Joe gets up. Joe fishes in his pocket for money.)

JOE:

Still a quarter, right, Park? It'll be a sad day when you have to raise your prices. Damned hard times! FDR HAS to change our economy or we'll ll be selling apples on Salina St. Imagine... those folks trying to sell apples to keep from panhandling. A man needs his dignity!

PARK:

Yup, still two bits. Guess a barber in Syracuse has raised his price for a cut to 40 cents. BUT, there are several barbers competing for customers on Salina St. Here, it's just little "o'l me in little o'l Funnyville". Thought of raising my prices some but it's just too hard on folks. Be right with you, Frank. Hey- have a good day Joe. and say hello to your sweet Martha. Bye.(Joe exits as Frank gets in chair. Park does a quick sweep of the hair on the floor. Ad libs.) And what can Figaro do for you today?

FRANK:

Yes, sir! The usual. Shave the neck and cheeks and trim the beard. BOY! No one shaves as close as you do, Park. And I don't need to worry about you slitting my throat! Do I?? And the hot towel is so relaxing. Feels great! Ah, this damned Depression! Too many stories of people going under and now they have nothing. Imagine the farmers out west. no crops... just wind and blowing dirt and dust. Where can they go?

PARK:

You said it. The other day I shaved a gent... gave him a final cut too at Eaton's Funeral Home. He didn't complain! Poor fella killed himself- lost it all in the stock market. His wife and kids have nothing. The Masonic brothers are covering the funeral expenses. We need to discuss what the family will go through now that he is gone. They need help... we just can't leave them.

FRANK:

Certainly we can discuss this at the lodge at Thursday's meeting. These days, they're listing the cause of death as "accidental" but people know the truth.

PARK:

Suicide! The family's pain must be horrible. The ladies of the Methodist Church are tending to visitation, food and such. He had 3 little ones... A terrible loss! We step up and help, especially with the hell people are going through.

LOUIE (Enters):

Hey, Parker- need a quick trim. Gotta go for a job this afternoon.

FRANK:

Great... a job! Then you must be in a hurry. Suppose we let Park do you now? Then you can get to that job. Meanwhile I can relax a tad longer in our own Boy's Club. No women here! (They all laugh).

PARK:

If that's alright with you.. (Nods. Park shakes off the cover as Frank gets out of the chair. Louie takes the chair. Frank holds the towel on his face and sits in a customer's chair.)

LOUIE:

Gee, that's mighty nice of you, sir. The job is haulin' rocks to build stone fences in farmers' fields. Boy- those fences will last a lifetime... or more. It's paid for by good ol' Uncle Sam. It's a job! Don't want to have to join those guys on street corners asking for hand outs. 'Buddy, can you spare a dime?' NO sir- I hope I won't have to do that. I got my pride. I can't beg. This here Civilian Conservation Corps is giving work to folks like me.

FRANK:

Well, I've got time. The bank can wait-there aren't too many customers these days anyway. They're all running the other way. It's good that you are willing to do that physical labor and you're strong. A man needs to be working. They need laborers to build the Empire State Building and the Golden Gate Bridge. Imagine these being built in our lifetime! Keeps men employed!

LOUIE:

You bet! It'll pay enough to help me and my family for a while anyway. Damn- these lean, mean years had better be over soon! I come to this country in 1928 because of jobs and equal opportunity for everybody. Times is tough in Europe too. Say, Park- you always have that long-hair music playing. You like that music, huh?

FRANK:

My man, I'll have you know that Parker Gladden is an accomplished musician- fine trombone player. He also composes music. (Blank face on Louie). He writes it! You should hear his music sometime.

PARK:

Wish I'd applied myself more. Always seeing the fun side-a real wise ass! When I was 21... I went to Finland with the Dana School of Music band. I was living in Ohio then. The school band was selected to go to Finland and play a series of concerts throughout the country. It was quite an honor! Like a darned fool, I fooled around not taking much of anything too seriously. In Helsinki, I met the incomparable Sebelius... a great composer. Anyway, I asked the old guy to pose for a photograph. I said I wanted to take many pictures of him. He was so sincere and happy that this young American wanted to take photos of him- I asked the old guy to pose this way and that... I monkeyed around like I was some great photographer. I thanked him. Then I whispered to my friend that I didn't have any film in the camera! There I was asking the old gent to strike dramatic poses for me - and I was out of film! And there he was, smiling all the time! Darned fool I was! I got a kick out of the old gent. Now I WISH I had all those pictures! Smart ass, I!... Say- I'll be playing at the Burnett Park this Saturday night. Bring the family. It's a free concert. The Syracuse Symphony starts at 7 PM. Bring the kids and they can have a great time running around as the music plays!

LOUIE:

Sure would like that! It'd be a great night out for the wife and the youngins. And the price is just right! (To Frank) Thanks mister. (He fumbles in his pocket for money)

PARK:

That's ok, Louie. You can owe me. No- I know what's better than money. I sure could use a couple of of your home grown squashes. The last one you gave me was a real beaut. Good thing you have that cellar to store all the potatoes and squashes. Wish my own garden was a plentiful as yours. You need to tell me your secret! Just read that folks in Appalachia are eating dandelions and berries. That's all. Poor kids. (pause) I hope you get the job. I want to see you smiling the next time I see you!

LOUIE:

You got it. No one grows da vegetables like us Paisanos! I bring you BEEG tomatoes and zucchini... lots of zucchini. You like da zucchini? You love jokes... here's one. Have to tell you... This poor Italian immigrant was in court for a traffic violation. He could not a speeek da EEEnglish much. So, the judge finished giving him his sentence. He says to the Paisan," Peace be with you!" And the Piasanne says to the judge, "Yeah. And a lotta pees on you too, Sir, Judge". Get it? Caoi! (Laughter. goodbye ad libs as Louie exits. Frans climbs back in the chair and Park gets him set again).

FRANK:

He's a good man! You're a good man, Park!

PARK:

These rotten times makes everyone crazy. A man needs to be valuable. He needs to work and support his family. Darned few men have jobs.

FRANK:

You said it! How's your charming Miss Marie Hamilton doing? Haven't seen her around town in a while.

PARK:

She's in Brooklyn taking advanced nursing courses for her promotion to Charge Nurse at Crouse-Irving Hospital. She'll be away 6 months... 180 days too long! God, how I miss her so already!

FRANK:

Parker- we've been friends for a long time. Take my advice and marry the little woman. Amazing what the right woman can do for a man! Her father is Pastor Frank Hamilton, right? A real fire and brimstone preacher I understand! Really hard- boiled! Which church?

PARK:

Fayetteville Methodist... but he's finally retiring. But what an intelligent man... a preacher, a PHD in Religion... and a pharmacist! Imagine- all those degrees! An Elmer Gantry! I just smile in his presence! But Marie's mom is a wonderful lady- I really enjoy talking with her. Marie has her warming smile. And then there's her sister, Dorothy- she can be testy at times. And there's the brother, Charles. He doesn't approve of me at all... because of my drinking. But he's no Puritan... can't trust him too far... a bit of a womanizer, he is! Has his sights set on joining the Army and take charge of the canine corps. He's fond of German Shepherds... raises 'em. He was too young for WW1... the Big War. Let's hope that there'll never be another World War... Ever! Anyhoo... since he has a passion for dogs, he can't be all that bad! Good with dogs- and lousy with people.

FRANK:

Whoa! The mere mention of German. That Big War was enough for the U.S.! Today some Americans say it's unpatriotic to have a Dachshund or a German Shepherd... BECAUSE of the Germans! Darn shame- those dogs didn't ask to be bred in Germany! Beautiful and smart dogs! Anyway- back to Marie. Marry the lass! Been married to Maude for 36 years now! Good woman and I'm a lucky man! Marie will tame you, son! (Park has been readying him and shaving him.) Oh, I got to tell you... I've been using one of those new safety razors!

They're brand new! The razor pops out of the case. Kinda handy and I haven't cut myself once! But there's nothing like a good old fashion straight edge shave from The Barber of Funnyville! And these safety razors- the blades are disposable... just toss 'em away. What'll they think of next?

PARK:

What next? The idea - putting us barbers out of the shaving business! Saw them advertised in Sears catalog. Probably the older gents will continue to want a clean, professional shave with a straight edge! Sure hope so... I take great pride in my good scraping!

FRANK:

Right! The pampering is really relaxing! Changes! Progress! Before long we'll be allowing women to take men's jobs! Maybe they'll even start coming into a man's barber shop. Imagine a barber cutting both men's and women's hair? Both! Naw- a woman's place is in the home!

PARK:

Anyhoo... the times they are a changin'! The hospital would fire Marie if they found out that we got married. Sort of like school marms and librarians. They want 'em single and devoted to their work! Marie loves being a nurse- pediatrics especially! She loves kids!

FRANK:

O. then she'd love to have kids of her own, right, Park? Keep her at home and take her shoes away from her! (They laugh.)

PARK:

PARK:

I've promised her I'd stop boozing... and I've been real good. I just get so depressed. My dad is hardly well enough to tend to the Manlius shop... so I need to cover for us both. Heck- listen to me going on and on. There are worse off folks. There, all set, Frank! (Frank pays Park, gives him a Masonic handshake and they exchange small talk.)

FRANK:

I feel great! And give my regards to your dad. (They exchange small talk. Frank gives Park the Masonic handshake and Frank exits. Park sweeps some. Gets paper and pen, sits in chair and writes.)

VOICE OVER, PARK:

Dearest Lizzie: Time for my noon repast! Shall break for lunch to have some of that bunny Fetteroff gave me yesterday... no doubt I'll be leaping and bounding all over town shortly! Shall post this so you will have some of my foolishness to read soon. So, cheerio for now! Don't forget, sweetheart, I'm missing you. Must be love! Are you glistening? Love and kisses, Park. PS. Honey-Good luck... the best of success to you!

SCENE: 4 days later. Music up. Blackout. We hear Parks' voiceover. Lights gradually come up in the nurse's station where Marie is seen reading the letter.

VOICE OVER, PARK:

Dearest Lizzie: It is now a whole week since you left! Gee- my Marie-your name MIGHT have been Elizabeth Marie as well as Marie Elizabeth. So there! Your big fat letter arrived and I nearly devoured it! I feel so inspired after reading such a sweet letter. Yesterday afternoon I became so busy at 4 and they kept coming til 9... I didn't even have time to eat! I was so tired that I drove to Manlius and ordered 4 bottles of Janack's beer. Then I was in bed by 11:30. Boy- o boy- I sure am blue! If I could write words as readily as I write music, I'd send lots of songs to you. But, dammit-the words don't come out! Your beloved brother

came in yesterday and gave me a toot of that TNT-homemade hooch.
Tasted awful! He was asking me what news I had of you... (fade. Then
we see Marie in the nurse's station)

MARIE (Nurse's Station... reading letter):

This powerful "Katrina" who is your Ruler... must be an immense
woman. Guess you'll need to listen to her! (Or she may sit on you!
Smiles!) She sounds like some character out of a Wagnerian opera-horns,
braids and all! About the hat you saw! Talk about dreams... I WILL
have on a different chapeau when we meet next. Won't that be lovely?
I have to keep my eye on this old brown one that you and mom hate.
Mom keeps threatening to burn it! Have to keep this short as I expect
customers. Suppose everyone is getting set for the big election. Guess
who I'll vote for? A hint- his name starts with R. After I shaved Mr.
Beach at 1 pm, I dropped by your house. They were all in the midst of
their Sabbath repast. Your mom told me she heard from you and I told
her SOME of the contents of your recent letter. Only some! I could not
get into the mushy stuff... LOVE THOSE WORDS, HONEY! Your
ma invited me to eat but I had to decline. They all looked the same.
By gosh- with you away, my interest just wasn't. At 3 pm I laid down
on the davenport and I turned on the radio and listened to the Boston
Pops. You guessed it- I didn't hear much of it as I fell asleep! At 8, my
dad and I went into town to the Strand to see "Goona, Goona" and also
"Virtue" with Carole Lombard and Pat O'Brian. I liked "Virtue" loads.
It was an exact duplicate of the night we went into the Strand- rained
like hell when we went in and more rain-hell when we got out! Dearest-
shall take this to the post office and inquire if I have any mail from my
'ittle Nurtz! All my love... ever thinking of you! Park

(BLACKOUT. Tipsy music is heard. "Show Me the Way to go
Home" or similar. Car screeches to a stop, car doors shut and Park and
Hottie laugh as evening lights are up. They slowly and sloppily approach
the shop. They are drunk. It is 2 am. They both laugh heartily and
drunkenly.)

HOTTIE: (drunkenly)

Some night! Our heads will be heavy tomorrow! Whew! Guess I need to try to walk home - let the damned car just sizzle there. (Park fumbles with keys to the door as he tries to open the shop door. Drops them. They both twitter. Eventually, Park opens it and he falls into the shop.)

PARK:

Yup. You do... doodle that. How'd we even make it here? Some hooch! No More! No more!! I'm gunna sleep it off here fore I head home. My old man will be mad as hell with me! Yeah. yeah.(Sings "Animal Fair", giggles. Steadies himself against the barber chair. The street light streams through the window, the only light. Park with great effort plops into the barber chair. Reaches for Marie's photo on the counter.)

PARK: (Speaks to the mirror)

Ahhh, damn it! Said I would NOT drink.. and... and... and Marie... My Marie (Starts dancing around singing "My Marie".) If only you were here with me to keep me away from the demon rum! (He turns the radio on; "Stardust" is playing. Park tears up and babbles.) Cannot go home like this. No- sir-ee. Ah, hell- a man deserves to have a little TOOT now and then. Oh, Honey! Honey! I'm sorry! I'm so sorry! (weeping) Ah.. hell... just rest up here a bit before I go home. Ah, cripe! What a louse! You stinkin' louse! (Wanders into the back room and gets his trombone Re-enters playing a rag and dances about. He is still good. even drunk! Finally, he puts down the horn and burps! He pulls out Marie's last letter and starts reading.)

(Lights up in Nurses' Station as Marie enters. Muted hospital PA calls. She writes in a patient's chart. Looks around for Head Nurse and sees no one.)

MARIE: (writing and reading)

Just think. Only 9 more weeks left here. I believe you when you say you will try not to drink. Parker, you become someone else when you drink. I understand that you feel so terrible because of your father's poor health. It's not fair that you are the only bread-winner in the family now... but you can do it! I wish I could hold you close right now when you get lonely and so upset. I miss your funny face, your dumb jokes... your warm kisses. My Darling- I have to go now but I am thinking of you and I KNOW you will be strong. I love you, darling. Be good til I see you. I LOVE you and miss you awfully. Marie (She puts the letter in an envelope, seals it with a kiss. Enter Katrina)

KATRINA: (German accent)

Miss Hamilton! I find you out at this station too much! Our work is never done... the patients always need our attention. There is no time for breaks! I suggest that you tend to the patient in room 215... NOW! Ah- there is my pencil! (Pick up pencil and stares at Marie.)

MARIE: (Taking the patient's chart and exiting)

Yes. Right away, Miss Algermisson.

(Fade out. Music. Lights up on nurse's station. reveal of Marie pulling Park's letter from her pocket. She looks around to be certain that she isn't being watched. She opens the letter and reads that Park "fell off the wagon". She shows her disappointment just when Big Nurse (Miss Algermisson) walks by. Marie quickly folds her letter and puts it in her pocket.)

MARIE:

Good Morning, Miss Algermission.

KATRINA:

(with a big "humph"; she smiles evily and stands staring a moment. She then walks briskly to Marie.) Miss Hamilton- this is a hospital- a teaching hospital! Keep your personal material at home, not in the workplace. This is no place for your musings! You are to be Florence Nightingale.. a Clara Barton and you must always be on task. Your personal life must not interfere with your duties. Am I making myself clear? We cannot tend to our patients when we have our nose in a letter, can we now?

MARIE:

No, Miss Algermission. I'll tend to them right now. Oh, I need to ask you about the patient in room 204. He was asking for you. I believe that you wrote this last entry. (She checks chart and tray of meds)

KATRINA:

Yes, patient Miller. I will check on him before I leave my shift today. He tells me that you are most kind to him. You DO show promise, Miss Hamilton. I am trying my best to make you into an exemplary Charge nurse. Sometimes we must put away our emotions.

MARIE:

I feel so close to my patients and each one is so very special. Gee- I've gotten to know their families too... and I understand. It's just that I so enjoy getting letters from home... I've been here several weeks now.. and I...

KATRINA: (cutting her off)

I understand that you are somewhat lonely. Away from your family and loved ones. But, in essence you are married to your profession when you become a nurse. You have been told that you, as head nurse, cannot be married. That is the policy of hospitals. Many others would love to have the educational opportunity that you now have. You may have to make up your mind. Those are the rules. And, do not become too close to your patients, Miss Hamilton. Now, take inventory of the medications. (Katrina spins and walks away as Marie gives her a disgruntled look.)

SCENE: Barber shop. Park has 4 customers. Ed Eastman is chewing tobacco and spits regularly in the spittoon, Park is brushing the hair off Teddy, a young man, retarded. There are many locks of hair on the floor signifying that Park has been busy.)

PARK:

(Singing and doing a little dance) "Shave and a haircut- 2 bits" (All laugh.) Teddy, you always sit so still for your haircut. Audience mine. Let me sing a song for you that I wrote. We're all going through these horrible times. Here goes: (Parker clowns around as he sings) [Note: This music composition of Park Gladden's is scored and available to use.]

The fella on whom the taxes fall, is you
You whose salary check is small,
whose luxuries are few.
Robbing the rich of their every cent
Won't pay a third of the billions spent.
The burden-bearer of government - is you!

2nd verse- Ain't no better, ain't no worse...

The farmer, laborer, salesman clerk-you pay
Out of the wages for which you work,
A quarter is drained away-
By hidden taxes on board and bed-
the clothes you wear and the food you're fed.
From your beginnings until you're dead-You pay!

Make no mistake if he rich went broke, still you-
Would stagger under the heavy yolk that's breaking your back in two!
Though super taxes would pay the bill of every factory, store and mill-
Still YOU- you're liable to pay the bill that's due!

And, if this squandering does not halt-
The average citizen - whose at fault?

It's YOU! It's YOU!
(All applaud. Laugh)

TEDDY:

You make me laugh, Mr. Parker. I like that song!

PARK:

I thought you'd like it, me fine fellow! Zippy, huh? (Teddy tries to pay attention as they chat!)

LEROY:

Lookin' good, Parker. Damn government anyway! Time for FDR to step up and FIX this country!

FRANK:

Yup! You need to let everyone hear your song... Let everybody hear it! So true. Roosevelt MUST shape up America!

PARK:

For starters, I'll be singing it at the Elks Club variety show- next Saturday! I'll be dressed as a tramp. At least it'll get a premiere! Park- the hobo!

TEDDY: (pulling on Park's sleeve)

What you mean when you say hobo?

PARK:

You've seen those guys camping out at the railroad tracks? Those are tramps... hobos. They have no homes... just kickin around. Mostly hop on railroad cars and go onto the next place. It's like a special club. They've got a great way to help out other hobos-when they want to give a sign to other hobos that this house or that house will be kind and them

food, work... a place to sleep. Then they carve... maybe a cat, on a tree
telling others that in this house is a good woman, etc.

FRANK:

Great signals! Cripe! That could be anyone of us! Gotta help out
each other.

TEDDY:

Mr. Parker- you gunna go into the city today? My mama wants
you should take me into the city if you're goin! I would love to ride in
your big black car, Mr. Parker... so, Mr. Parker... you going to the city
today? (Customers are used to Teddy. One snickers as others give him
that "shut up" look; others are reading)

PARK:

Teddy... you tell your mom that I may be going in tomorrow. I
would be glad to take you with me. I'll call her later this afternoon.
how's that?

TEDDY:

(To the others) Mr. Parker a good friend. He take me with him. See
you soon, Tank you. Tank you. Gotta go now, Mr. Parker. Hair look
real good! Gonna sing that silly song you taught me. You sing too, Mr.
Parker. (Park coaches him through the song)
    I'm goin' to town to smoke my pipe,
    I won't be back 'til Saturday night.
    If you should let the old witch in,
    I'll clonk you on the head with a rolling pin!
    I might as well do it now- CLUNK! CLUNK!

(He laughs as he clunks Parker on the top of his head. Ted waves
as he exits. He exits fully)

ALL: ad lib "byes"

FRANK:

You certainly have a lot of patience, Parker. You're so kind the poor boy. Such a shame... that car accident left him so mangled in the head. Teddy will always have the mind of a 6 year old. Poor boy must be in his early twenties now. A lousy accident like that could happen to anybody. Any of us. His folks are real good people, too. At least he can get around on his own. He couldn't ever hurt a soul! (Reads from paper) Says here," Out of 25,000 US banks, there are just 11,000- victims of the Depression. Folks have no faith in the system. The Runs on the banks finished them off. This and the Crash in '29 bring no positive...

(Lights fade to dark in shop; gradually lights up in the nurses' station. We see Marie finishing writing her letter. She blows her nose in her hanky. Sneezes. She has a cold) She spots Katrina and conceals the letter in her uniform pocket. Katrina walks by noticing her condition.

KATRINA:

Miss Hamilton-I suggest that you get some chicken soup... and some sleep. We cannot have a nurse with a cold around our patients, now, can we?

MARIE:

Yes. I seem to have caught a cold. May I leave by 4 this afternoon? Just one hour early. I promise I'll get some rest.

KATRINA:

You do know that that presents a burden on our other staff. BUT, we are a hospital and we cannot have you being sick and ministering to our patients! (Marie starts to leave.) WAIT, Miss Hamilton! I must say that I am most pleased with your work... and your attention to details. You have a charming smile and are at ease with the patient. Your monthly evaluation is stellar! (She takes a folder and reads from the papers in it.) Appearance- excellent. Keep those shoes very white! Knowledge of material - excellent! I am astounded by your scholarship! Patient care- excellent! They seem to ask for YOU... which is good. Handling difficult situations- - excellent. You seem so calm even in an emergency setting. I have written up a scenerio of your involvement with the cholicy baby. He might have died if you hadn't known just what to do. Commendable! My... I'd say you are on your way to becoming an excellent charge nurse! Keep up the promising work! (She drops the toughness and pats Marie's hand and exits. LIGHTS OUT as Marie takes her letter and reads.)

VOICE OVER (PARK):

Gee, honey... so sorry to learn that you aren't feeling quite yourself. So happy to learn that Katrina the Witch has given you an excellent evaluation. The world is in need of better and brighter people and I'm happy to know that BIG NURSE isn't as nasty to you anymore! Now- if you can't make it home for Christmas- maybe I can come there. Every other Saturday there are excursions to New York City via the Lackawana Railroad - round trip $4.50. Train leaves Syracuse terminal at 10PM and gets to the City by 6 AM. Leaves again Sunday night. It would give us a few hours. Jeepers, am I dreaming? We will make some plans to be together for a wee bit anyway. Darn it! There are too many miles between us! Business has been dead. Let's hope things pick up after Roosevelt takes the wheel. Meanwhile, more tough old pickings for the rest of us. (Lights fade in the station and up full in the shop.) Wish you were here for Sunday dinner. Maybe we cook 'em nice chick! Hmmm- we cook 'em funny- take feathers off - stick in pot - eat much. and get sick da hell! So much for Tony's humor today! O, did I tell you that I love you and I miss you sooooo much! Love, Park.

End ACT 1

ACT 2

(Shop. Hotty enters, as always, rushed. He shakes off snowflakes.)

PARKER:

Hey, puppy dog!

HOTTIE:

What's your story, morning glory? Say, Park- just comin' in from the cold! Just finished fixin' Sam's car... doubt he'll be able to pay me... NOBODY can pay!

PARKER:

I still owe you 75 cents for that headlight! I should be able to pay you in a couple of days.

HOTTIE:

Say- you need to step out tonight. (Spits a huge wad of tobacco in the spittoon.) I know a place where we wouldn't be stuck with that legal beer! Legal beer- ha- that stuff is all watered down and no guts! None of that Pickwick ale! Whaddya say?

PARKER:

Nope! I promised Marie that I'd be a good boy! And I am- most of the time.

HOTTIE:

Just located a peachy Plymouth! You keep talking about a ride to Boston to visit your sister... you can borrow this car! Can you handle all that power? And maybe I can go along, too?? Loads of sights to see in Baaaaaaaston!

PARKER:

When my sister, Gen, and her husband visited us this past summer, it was too much. You know- Confucius say "fish and visitors smell different after 3 days! And they were here for a week!

HOTTIE:

Yeah- and Confucius also say, "Crowded elevators smell different to midget."

PARKER:

Their vacation was over. But for me, it was over the minute the princess arrived! Ah- I guess it was good having the "Princess Genevieve" here. She and I always get on each other's nerves. Hmm... some of us working stiffs never get a vacation! I have a PAYING job at the Onondaga Hotel Friday night- pays $8. I'll bet my sis would love to cut the rug there, So... NOOOOO... Hotty- I Will not go out with you Friday! By the way, saw Roy coming out of Chubs' late yesterday afternoon. Betcha he had a toot or 2 in there! Burned me up when he told Marie's mom about the other night! The knocker!

HOTTIE:

A man deserves to let loose now and then. Guess you won't be telling him any of YOUR secrets! Huh?

PARKER:

You bet! I smell a snake! The snitch! He gets tipsy a lot but he tattles on me!

HOTTIE:

Gotta get some lunch. Maybe the diner - they really pile it on for me there. One babe - well endowed (gesture)- has the sweets for me. Must be my manly charms!

PARKER:

O sure... you brute! Yup- I just had a magnificent lunch myself- stringed beans, cold beef and ice tea. Better than any restaurant lunch, even if I COULD afford one!

HOTTIE:

Have ta laugh. when I checked out your car yesterday, you didn't have no gas! No gas! That could be why it ain't runnin' so good. Then I check them tires. And, right before my eyes- the right front tire exhaled! POOF! Right before my eyes- it just sank!

PARKER:

So, how much for a tire these days?

HOTTIE:

A new one will run you $4- $4.50. But I can get you one for 2 bucks. How's that?

PARKER:

Guess so... need to put the car up... I hardly need it now that Marie isn't here. No need to drive her to and fro Crouse Irving Hospital. I can take the bus. Can I keep my car at your place?

HOTTIE:

Sure. I can park it behind the garage for you. Spring is right around the corner. Maybe the price of gas will be down by then. When is Marie due?

PARKER:

Due? Due? No- she's not pregnant! (Laughs) Early March. For me, every day is forever! (He shouts) I LOVE THAT WOMAN! Hotty- we've been friends for a long time. (Park starts walking Hotty out the door) But you gotta stop coming by. I've made up my mind that will NOT go drinking with you. Stay friends - yes - but no more drinking buddies. You hear?

HOTTIE:

Sure. Sure! You're reformed... again! (Hottie just stares at him and exits. BLACKOUT!)

PARK- VOICE OVER:

My Little Buttercup: Today is December 5th. Just opened for business and your sweet letter arrived. A real nice one, honey! Thanks so much! Looks like big horse Katrina sort of cares for you, baby. Guess we cannot judge another by the size! Look at the elephant... not nearly as harmful as a little bug. Jeepers- I'm bugs about you, baby!

Last night I drove to the Regent to see "Red Dust" with my dad. I really enjoyed it! Dad's friend was home and offered me some homemade "hooch". When I said, "NO!" my dad nearly collapsed. I am still high up on the wagon. I don't want to fall from this height. Had salmon for lunch and this may sound a bit fishy, but it's true! A gloomy rainy morning. and dark. I could have remained 'neath the quilts a wee bit longer! This cold morning here- my toe hurts. Wish you were here to bandage it up and make it all better. I put some of your zinc oxide on it tho, just like my little nursie told me to. Don't know how many pounds I've lost since you left but I'll admit, I'm so damned lonesome! You and I always got along, right? When we didn't, it was my fault or rather the fault of wine. We WILL have some nicer times... someday... somewhere... somehow... Well, I must put a penny stamp on this and mail it to you. Love and Kisses- Park

SCENE: Barbershop. Lights full. Park is BUSY! Frank, Sully, Louie, Fred Quakenbush and Joe are waiting for Park. One reads the newspaper; one gets up to spit in spittoon, one smokes and Fred is nervously looking out the window.

PARKER:

Dad went up to the Manlius shop this afternoon. He was helping mom with the laundry this morning. I might have had that job but I was afraid it might give me too much experience- might prove too handy at a later date. Maybe baby diapers. oh gee. You can never tell... the women are commencing to wear the pants... we poor males must do something about this soon! Maybe men will wear the skirts!

(Fred spots what he's looking for and says, "Ah, Shit!" and he ducks into Parks' backroom. Park is cutting the fourth customer's hair when we see Mrs. Quakenbush. (She looks a great deal like Marjorie Main from "Ma and Pa Kettle". A terror!) We see her walk back and forth outside the window. She is apparently looking for something or someone.)

MRS. QUAKENBUSH: (opening door)

Have any of you skunks seen my no good husband? (They all shrug their shoulders and play dumb.) She walks about the shop, sniffing. She mutters, "That no good..." as she exits and slams the door.

(Fred re-enters from the backroom and all the guys laugh. Fred waltzes over to the mirror and checks as he laughs. Just then. Mrs. Quakenbush bursts in through the door and towers over him. She grabs him by the collar.

MRS. Q:

There you are, you no good... SOOOOO, you're wasting time at your boys' club. You're supposed to be looking for a job. Get down to that mill - now! (He tries to get away but she collars him and they head out the door. DEAD SILENCE! Men look at one another. Ad libs follow)

LEROY:

Ha! No rest for the wicked! She got him! Damn- that has to be embarrassing.

FRANK:

Did you see the look on Fred's face when she stormed in? He was as white as a skeleton. The only thing she was missing was a rolling pin! (Laughs)

PARKER:

I know he has no money. He wasn't in here for a cut, that's for sure. Guess he escaped from the paper mill for a few minutes... IF he ever got down there!

LEROY:

Married to THAT battle-axe... who would want to stay home? I'd stay at work rather than go home to that!

PARKER:

Gotta check the mail. (He goes out to get mail. Re-enters and thumbs through letters/bills) Yep, that gets filed. (He places bill in drawer then beams as he discovers Marie's letter and carefully opens it. Guys snicker.) Gents- I've been waiting for word from Marie after her nasty bout with the flu. And, it 'tis! Just a minute whilst I inhale this this delicious letter! (He sniffs letter for perfume.) Hmm... smells more like hospital disinfectant! Just the same - this is good. (He reads to himself and smiles!) She LOVES me!! (Cat cries and adlibs from guys. "Lucky guy!","And the price of stamps these days.")

SULLY:

That's the kind of gal to have... far away!

LEROY:

So, when is Marie due home?

PARKER:

She says she'll be home for good in March. Darn... what a long, cold winter this has been without my Armstrong heater! I am SO proud of her! When she returns, she is assured of her supervisory position at Crouse-Irving Hospital... head of Pediatrics! She asked about the marathon dances here- says they're plentiful all over New York City!. the craze everywhere!

FRANK:

I hear that there are only 4 couples still standing at the dance hall in Kirkville. The rest of the couples that started 5 days ago dropped out. 2 were hospitalized! And talk about crazy- Crazy bastards are sitting on blocks of ice and eating ice cream at the same time in Chicago! All for prize money!

PARKER:

Some entertainment! Kooks! I wouldn't mind stumbling around the dance floor as long as my Marie would hold me up! Looks like the human race will soon be apes again. Ah. the human race... wonder who'll win?

(Enter Robert (a) with armful of shoes! 2 pair are around her neck.)

ROBERT (A):

LOOK! Look! A truck carrying a huge load of shoes just missed his turn at the bottom of East Genesee St. hill., The thing tipped over and off flew all the shoes! All kinds! They're everywhere! The driver wasn't hurt - he walked away- but people are scrambling everywhere for the shoes. You'd better hurry if you want to pick up some shoes. Better go get 'em! (Customers scramble out the door with ad libs: "Maybe I can get my kid a pair", "Hope I find my size", "Don't care what size-", "Hell -I'll give 'em away if they don't fit.", etc. Frank stays.

BLACKOUT in shop. Nurse' s station lights up. Reveal. We see Marie writing in a patient's chart. Hospital noises are muted. She writes Park a letter)

MARIE (writing/reading):

Dear One- you keep me smiling. Thank you! It's almost Christmas. This is such a long winter and I've been kept real busy. I long for a simple evening with you- just you! A movie would be fine but we needn't go anywhere. The days are long here in this busy hospital. And, brother- do my feet ever hurt! I can handle the workload, but Ms. Algermisson keeps me in the edge all the time. I hope that I can take the good that she is teaching me and never emulate the negatives. Namely her!!! I believe that she cares - BUT she is so harsh. Sometimes my feelings are hurt too easily... you've told me that. I wish I had a better... sense of humor like you! Right now, I'd like nothing better than to spend the afternoon with just you at the Swan Pond. We could do nothing... and I would love that!... only 6 weeks more and (sound and lights fade out. Barber Shop LIGHTS UP. Park is sitting in his chair writing the letter. We hear Park's VOICE OVER.)

PARKER (voice over):

Gee, honey girl. I slipped off the wagon Saturday night. I went up to Manlius, picked up my dad and then re-turned home. Then I thought I'd go to Manlius Center and watch the Marathon dancers again. First, I decided to go over to that speakeasy behind our house for some "tuning up". That was some of the darndest gin I've ever had! At first I got a ½ pint, sat there and consumed it. Then, not satisfied, I ordered another ½ pint. Time sped on and all of a sudden it was 1 am. I knew the dance would be over and I suppose I had a little more after that. Then the first thing I knew, I didn't know anything! When I got home, Mom couldn't coax me to go to bed. Her temper got the best of her and she started to beat me with her broom. Then she got my poor dad into it. I guess we clinched and wrestled. I know he had me by the neck once and I broke the hold by pressing my elbow into his chest. Well, Sunday I woke up and I could barely walk with my left foot bruised by that broom. My neck has a deep scratch down it, about 5 inches long. Boy! It must have been a terrible battle! MY ills are over but dad thinks I broke one of his chest bones! He hasn't been feeling well anyway- I wish I had been the one to receive the worst of it. That damned booze-I hope I've had enough. If mom used her head, I would have gone to bed quietly. But she gets so excitable! Damn it- I am so ashamed of myself. Please know that I am such an ass! Geepers, honey- you don't know how sorry I am. It's a wonder you haven't left me flat the way I drink and all before seeing you. You must be very patient or else you care for me alot. I am sorry for everything! I realize it's up to me to pull myself back up. This, I shall try to do. Please believe me. Geepers, "A Sweetheart is Forever" (or "Stardust") is playing on the radio... WSYR. That makes me sad. So many tunes remind me of your, honey. Gee, do you notice I'm getting all these GEES and GEEPERS from you? Love it, honey! I AM being good- about other women, that is. I slipped the other way- and I am sorry. Watch those doctors now- remember what the fortune teller said. All my love--and REAL too, Park. (Fade out; music up then away.)

(Park enters shop)

PARKER

(In shop, Park slowly enters. Cleans mirrors, empties ashtrays etc. Turns sign to OPEN. Talks into the mirror.) Park! you MADE it! Pull yourself together. And, don't be a shithead today. (Turns on radio. Gets paper and pen and writes. Laughter outside and he goes to the window to see. Mrs. Hamilton and Dot are laughing but not seen. Hamilton walking by. He opens the door and invites them in... possibly just Dot)

PARKER:

Top of the morning to yee, Miss Mademoiselle Dorothy Hamilton! Entre! Entre! Mademoiselle...

DOROTHY: (entering the shop)

Good morning, Parker! Such a brisk morning! In Marie's last letter, she wanted me to remind you about the Methodist Church supper tonight. I know how much you enjoy the food.

PARKER:

Say-I wouldn't miss it for anything! Sure would love to have Marie come with me. Guess I'll have to eat enough for the two of us. (Laugh) Have you made your delicious cole slaw again?

DOROTHY:

Mother has roped me into helping out again this year. Usually Marie helps out- but not this year as she is away. Maybe I could be a good cook like Marie. Mother tells me that cooking well could land me a fine husband... you know -the way to a man's heart is through his stomach. (She giggles snottily)

ROBERT (A): (Entering quickly)

Morning, Mr. Gladden. Look. See what they're giving away free with every ticket sold to see "The Mummy" (She holds up a Depression Era vase.) And the movie was good too. I know how you like good movies so I wanted to tell ya. The movies was really scary but my cousin, Adam, is scarier looking than that!

DOROTHY:

Hello, Roberta. Gracious what strange looking glass. Who would want pressed ugly glass like that! it's so... so... ugly!

ROBERT:

I LIKE it! I'll give it to my mom. She collects everything. Sure looks like a dumb bowl to me! Maybe if Mom saves it it'll be worth something someday! Huh?

DOT:

That could be. It's odd to think that this Depression we are in right now will someday be history. It can't last much longer - Roosevelt says so! Keep it... and perhaps one day you'll be old and gray and remember where and when you got that thing. Well- I must be on my way to run errands. Mother feels strange about walking into a barbershop- not a lady-like thing to do. So, she's waiting for me on the corner. You do understand that she does send her "good day" to you but a LADY cannot be seen in a man's establishment. (She saunters over to the spittoon) Such a disgusting smell! (She spins and leaves) Goodbye, Parker. (Park stands holding the door for her.)

PARK: (checking to be certain she is gone)

That little snot!

PARK (Voice Over):

Dearest Mickey. Yesterday morning my dad went to the doctors and learned that his sternum bone is broken! Doc strapped it in for him. I am sooo sorry! I wish it was my head instead. Damned booze-wish they'd never discovered how to make it! My dad told Doc that he got fooling around. Please never mention the real incident to anyone. He DID have a strangle hold on me though. I had to get free. If it could have been someone other than my dad, it wouldn't hurt so much. There are alot of birds I'd like to crunch. Gee- he coughs so much I know I must have hurt him. I'll remember not to squeeze you too tight when we meet again! Monday, dad and I went into Syracuse. He went to the Eckle and I took in Keiths where I saw "I Am A Fugitive" with Paul Muni. Gee, it was thrilling! I don't believe I ever want to become a chain gang member. Hey- only 41 days til you're home. A mere drop in the bucket. Honestly, Fayetteville and this hard work are killing me by the inches. Trying to manage both barbershops and worrying about what I did to my Dad have me so stressed. Honestly, I feel like I murdered my dear old dad. It's the first thing I think about when I awake mornings; it shan't ever happen again! (Hottie is at the door. Leroy is sitting. Frank is in the chair.) Here comes business -must close.

HOTTIE:

Hey, Park. How about a trim?

PARK:

Darn you, Hottie! You're bad news whenever you come around. Bad... bad puppy dog! NO. NO. I WILL NOT GO DRINKING WITH YOU! Just a cut, right?

HOTTIE:

Ya know, Park you worry too much. You need to relax more.

PARK:

I promised I wouldn't drink! I just HAVE to change this lousy habit. And YOU don't help much!

HOTTIE:

Hey- everybody deserves to unwind. Why be depressed in this Depression? (Phony laugh) Say- I got that headlight for your car. Found a wrecked car and salvaged the thing for you. Won't cost you a thing... 'cept maybe a pint.

PARK

You know Charles- Marie's brother. He stopped in yesterday. I tried to lighten up a bit. That guy is a chore to converse with. I tried to lighten up the conversation. I lowered his ears some- of course - he had no money! I just smiled and told him that I'm looking out for Marie's baby brother!

HOTTIE:

You were going to tell me what happened at the funeral parlor past week.

PARK:

Jeepers! Never been so frightened. Gotta hear this! So, I was called to Eaton and Tubbs Funeral Home to cut the hair of a newly deceased patron. And also give him his final close shave.

FRANK:

Yes - you mentioned something about it before.

PARK:

So, Seldon said to go right in as he was busy. There was this poor dead fella. I didn't know the bloke - all laid out on the gurney in his birthday suit. Just a sheet over him. I thought to myself: "Self- YOU can do this!" So, I got my gear ready and I began to trim his hair. The fella's head was resting on a block type thing. Well- as I was all alone in the room, I really began to talk to myself saying it was ok. Really. He sure looked dead- lips were blue and he just lay there. Seldon hadn't worked his make up magic yet. Well, I was moving his head from side to side to get the clippers to do the base of his neck. And, IT happened. The bloke sat up! HE SAT UP! (Others react/adlibs) And there was this swooshing sound and gurgling coming from him. I turned tail and ran outta that room. Eaton ran after me as I was flying out that door and he started laughing. He put his hand on my shoulder and said, "SIT! Sit down! Get a hold of yourself!" He laughed some more. Damn, that was my first time cutting dead man's hair in a funeral parlor! After I calmed down, he told me that rigor mortis sets in and a body might just spring up for no reason. He told me about HIS first time dealing with this. He assured me that my bloke was good and dead! But- damn- it wasn't funny! I wet myself! (Guys react) He took me back to the prep room and showed me that he was really dead. I asked him to stay with me a while longer while I finished the job. He did. Eaton paid me and I was OUT of there! (All laugh, snicker, react) There's a first time for everything!

HOTTIE:

Damn! That's something! Don't know what I would've done... never had anything like that happen! I just deal with dead cars. (His haircut is finished. He leans into Park, whispering. Park smirks and shakes his head "yes". Hottie reaches into his pant's pocket and pretends to put a coin in Park's hand) Yup... gotta get to fixin' that damn car. (Or, Hottie says," Would you mind puttin' this on my tab?) Hottie exits.

PARK:

When he's sober, he's a darned good mechanic. Talk about hard times- his poor family... lost their homes. Had to move in with relatives for a while, he hopes. Reports say that over 1,000 homes a day are being taken back by mortgage holders. Darn shame. Even thousands of banks have closed their doors due to these hard times. It looks like most people are cutting their own hair at home to scrimp- way cheaper. Sure hope that I don't go out of business... reports from Syracuse say that several barbers are gone now. Sure is Starve the barber time! Hope I at least get business for Weddings... and funerals.

FRANK:

Leroy-I've been noticing that you've been rubbing your jaw. Are you alright?

LEROY:

My tooth has been killing me for a long time now! But I can't afford to go to no dentist. Without dough-you don't have that luxury of getting a real dentist take care of you! (Referring to the newspaper he's reading). More stories of long bread lines- mostly in the larger cities. Will Rogers says" (he reads): It's almost been Depression used to be a state of mind. Now it's a state of coma. Now it's permanent. Last year the President said, "Things can't go on like this'. They didn't... they got worse! (All laugh uneasily. He reads more) Hmmm. Stock market values plummet but... note this "US Steel, Gulf Oil, Shell Oil and General Motors empires are expanding!"

SULLY:

That's right. They're making out alright. On the backs of poor slobs like you and me.

PARK:

It's a darned good thing that people in this area have their own gardens. Too bad the winters are harsh... at least folks can grow their own veggies. Heck- how can you grow tired of carrots and beans? Everyone knows how to put up preserves and can vegetables. All these stories of folks who have lost it all. Imagine folks in New York City having to sell apples for a lousy nickel. Hope we don't need another war to get folks working again.

LEROY:

Says here that folks who've lost their homes and jobs have set up Hoovervilles! One big one in Chicago. They put the blame on Hoover for these hard times. Folks are living in boxes and any shelter they can find. Nothing much to eat, filth, no hope.

PARK:

Imagine all those people trying to survive together? A man needs his dignity! (Silence. All shake heads in agreement) I went by Mr. Beach's house and there was a crepe on the door. Guess the old guy has suffered his last.

FRANK:

My wife had been over there to help out. Now that he is gone, people will help out more. Good neighbors bring casseroles, and cakes and pies for the family. Thank God that people do care about each other here in our town. Guess undertakers won't lose THEIR jobs... no shortage of stiffs. OH- by the way I saw your mother-in-law to be today.

PARK:

Yup, I saw both Mrs. Hamilton and Dorothy as they were entering
the American Store. They both waved. I had to buy a new hat. Happy...
and my mom, too. Hated to part with the $3.50. But now I have good
brain protection! I searched and searched for my old hat but finally my
mother told me she burned it! Well, I liked it anyway!

LEROY:

Heard the other day that schools were shutting down- especially in
New York City. Can't pay their teachers! Darn, our kids need a good
education! They deserve more than the "school of hard knocks". The
kids are needed to work on farms and in canneries. And FDR promises:
"I pledge you! I pledge myself to a new deal for the American people!
"Roosevelt says that there'll be help for our young boys. Says here that,"
all boys 16 and will learn trades. They get $30 a month which allows
them to send some money home to their families. These kids might be
sent all over the US to learn trades. Darned few businesses are hiring-
just laying off good workers. Surviving at any cost! Hope Roosevelt
isn't just talking and promising what he can't deliver! Those damned
politicians!

FRANK:

I hear that many city kids are being put to work on farms... upstate-
-others are working in canneries and factories. Just to survive- families
have to split up. Never thought most families would have to move in
together... to economize. My mother-in-law keeps wanting to correct
Edna in the kitchen... but my wife keeps the peace. Imagine some
families having to live in small houses... very small castles!

LEROY:

OK. Hair looks good. It's getting late and I'd best be getting home.

(BLACKOUT as Voice Over comes up)

PARK, VOICEOVER:

My Darling Scottie waddy do! My Dearest Marie! Your dearest (and only) brother mooched a cut today. He said that he needed to look good for job interview. Heck-No one is hiring! Whose he kidding? So, what else is new? Saw your mom and she said that you were fighting a cold. Darned old throat germs anyway-- I could step on them and love it! Golly- took in $11 Saturday... not bad for a Saturday! Dad came home from the Manlius shop- all in- couldn't go a step further. He looked bad this morning-didn't attempt to leave the house. His bronchial trouble is worse-couldn't lie down but what he coughs his head off... he sits up in a chair all night. He hasn't been able to work all week- Guess he will have to give up the Manlius shop I fear. He sort of tottles when he walks. Darn- I feel so bad for him. I try to run up to Manlius to open that shop for a few hours. Dammit- I feel so upset about everything. Wish I could rule the world. There'd be no sickness! I've tried to get to bed early to guard my health. It would be bad if I were taken ill. Someone has to earn the bread and butter so I can't take any chances with my health. Sunday eve I was trying to slice off a leg of lamb, and carved myself instead. Gave myself a dirty cut on my forefinger so I drive up to Doc Sam's and he bandaged it for me. Old time is a-flying now- Only 8 days til Christmas... But who's counting? ME! Believe it or not, I haven't tasted alcohol for a whole week! My folks are so surprised- they don't know how to take it. Tell the truth- I was getting to the point where I felt so puck- I HAD to reform! With my dad sick and all, I can't afford to be taken sick. Sunday went to the Eckel to see "Sherlock Holmes" with Clive Brook. It was a treat as I haven't been to the movies in a while. GEEPERS, Hon- I LOVED the picture you sent! My 'ittle nursie looks so nice, gee whiz, I kiss the picture a lot! Ain't that nice?

(Lights up in barbershop. Park is sweeping hair when a lovely woman enters, Grace)

GRACE:

(looks Park over and evidently likes what she sees) Mr. Gladden- I'm Grace Stanton. I'm the hairdresser who spoke to you about renting space here.

PARK:

Yes. come in! (Grace wanders around the shop. Park definitely checks out her figure.)

GRACE:

As I mentioned, I'd like to rent space to use as a dressing parlor. Since I live in Manlius, this location is perfect for a beauty salon that could serve both Fayetteville and Manlius. I find it bothersome to have to head into Syracuse to set up shop and pay what they want. MY, My- it certainly looks like a barber shop!

PARK:

It IS a barbershop!

GRACE:

It could use a little decor... just a few touches.(Park studies her) Maybe some nice floral drapes... here and a pleasant smell. A spittoon!!? Thought those went out with the country folk! Must go...! Hmm, I don't see a phone. How on earth will people make appointments? Must have a phone.

PARK:

That's possible - but my clients know where I am. I don't want to think of that added expense of a telephone. Guess that would be about $3 a month to have one installed.

GRACE:

Sink? Where's the sink? There MUST be a sink for washing hair. (Park gestures to the back room) In there? (She parts the curtains and enters, then returns fast.) Oh, no- that won't do! I must have a sink out here in the shop! I am willing to give you 25% of my earnings. It seems like a fair rental for this space.

PARK:

Well... I'd want you to give me $15 a week... don't care for the percentage idea. Sorry- don't care for the added expense of running water lines and a telephone I'd need to pay for.

GRACE:

(Trying to seduce him.) But this is a trial. I don't know if the beauty shop will succeed here. Say- you know-I think you and I could get along famously. We could work well together!

PARK:

Suppose you let me think about this a while. I COULD use the extra income but then it would all change. MY customers are used to the way the place is... So am I.(He walks her to the door.) I'll let you know.

GRACE:

By Wednesday please- Let's see it's Monday now. I know you and I could work together very well.

PARK:

Ya know what. I'll decide now (Strongly!). The answer is NO! (She presses against him, he peels her off and gets her out the door. Park shakes his head. Leroy enters. Grace pokes her nose in the window all huffy)

LEROY:

Err. Err. have I come at a wrong time?

PARK:

NO! Thanks for the rescue. I've been trying to be polite. That lady wants to rent space here in the shop for her beauty parlor. I could use the added income but I had second thoughts about it. I was only THINKING about this business venture.

LeROY:

Hmm. A pushy woman, huh? But quite a looker! She can curl my hair... and my toes anytime! There'll be hell to pay if we emancipate them! This here's our SAFE SPACE- our gentlemen's club... away from women! A woman belongs in the home -barefoot and pregnant! (Laughs)

PARK:

Well- maybe not all that! I respect women who want to hold down a job... especially now. Everybody is doing what they can to survive. Most days I have to work like hell to keep up with the rents and so forth.
(Mrs. Hamilton and Dot are seen in the window walking outside. Park excuses himself and opens the door. They all chat briefly and the ladies go on their way. Park shuts the door.)

LEROY:

Say, Park... just wanted to drop in to tell you that there's a rehearsal for the Odd Fellows play- tomorrow night, 8 pm. Darn - you sure are funny as the nosey maid.

PARKER:

Don't know about my thespian pursuit! So, you like my portrayal? (ultra Southern) Mzzz Sally! And lookee at you- you're the sweet young thing! But if it'll help raise some money to help some folks out, glad to do it!

LEROY:

Then after the show we'll have some of that hard cider that Mack makes so well. A bit of hard cider on the back porch. Guess some of the women folk are planning a repast after the show.

PARK:

Fine! FINE! Thanks for stopping in. (Ad lib goodbyes. Park gets his pencil and paper and sits to write.)

VOICEOVER, PARK:

Gee. honey - it's starting to snow now... wish the rain, wind slush and snow would end- I'm so looking forward to the time when you and I can walk along in beautiful sunshine- happy balmy June evenings... sweet nothings whispered into each other's ears. Life sure would be awfully dull if we didn't have sweet dreams of the future. Would hate to think of what life would be like if we had nothing to wish for. Well, honey - I regret we cannot be together to see this old year out. Who needs 1932 anyway?! (LIGHTS fade in shop as lights bump up in nurses' station. We see Marie reading letter) Saw "Strange Interlude" at Loew's yesterday. With Clark Gable and Norma Shearer- just wonderful! What a strange story! In spots, the characters' thoughts are spoken in a voice-a new concept! You'd like that movie, my dearest! I regret that I didn't stay to see it a second time. Jeepers, I left Sunday dinner and drove up Genesee St. into Manlius, then drove down by your house for old time's sake. But when I got in front of Doc Badgley's, the darned car ran out of gas. I had a hellova time! But when I tried to push the ice was so bad I couldn't get my footing. Finally, I got past Tom Davis' house and coasted down the hill. See? All that for he love of my sweetest little girl! 'Scuse me for acting silly, but then- it's all in a lifetime! Last night, I stayed home, listened to the symphony program at 11, then - off to bed. Jeepers, this new sort of life is strange but I'm going to like it better as time rolls on! One thing is for certain, I feel better **because** I'm not drinking. I was on a stupid, wrong path... wish I had reformed sooner! Feel Tip Top! Hottie dropped in just as I was closing. His car isn't licensed either. So we walked up Genesee St. and down Elm. I went into the pool room and shot a few. Hottie waited for me and at 10:30 I went home. Hottie went home too! Ha! Looks as if I'm reforming him, too! You'll notice a difference in me when you get home. PROUD OF ME?? Dad went to the Manlius shop. He was helping mom with the laundry this morning. I might have had that job but I was afraid it would give me too much experience... might prove handy at a later date! Baby diapers... O gee. (Marie spots Katrina coming; hides letter)

KATRINA:

Miss Hamilton, You are here at the nurse's station much too frequently!- Have you tended to the afternoon Meds?

MARIE

Yes, I have. And everyone co-operated beautifully!

KATRINA:

Do not suppose that just because you have just 2 days left to your training that you can relax your attention to the work!

MARIE:

Miss Algermission- I have learned a great deal from you. I appreciate it all, I sincerely do. But why do you have to be so cold and unfeeling?

KATRINA:

What is meant by this? I AM your superior!

MARIE:

We have all tried to understand you! You preach that we must be compassionate to our patients. We all do that... quite well, in fact. However, you are the least compassionate of all the staff here and we do not understand why.

KATRINA:

No one has EVER spoken to me like that! Never! I do not need to defend my actions to you... or anyone else. I left my own country for a better life in the US. I worked hard to earn my RN degree. It has been most difficult for me- I took jobs that no one wanted to do- I cleaned, I cooked. I cleaned. I sent money back to my mother in Germany. And I paid for my training here. No one has EVER spoken to me as you have just now! I have half a mind to withdraw my excellent evaluation of your work!

MARIE:

I apologize for being so blunt... and hurtful. YOU are excellent at what you do. There must be warmth within you but I feel that you are hurtfully caustic... I pray that you will allow yourself to show the warmth that is in you... the warmth that each person needs.

KATRINA:

I try NEVER to show my feelings. And I do have them! It has been so hard for me... I know that you have a special male friend back home and his letters keep your spirit alive. I have no one but my work (at this Marie gives her a hug, Katrina cries. Finally Katrina steps back and looks at Marie.) You must NEVER let anyone know that I just received a special hug from you. And it was so good!! I thank you. After all-It would ruin my reputation! (Smiles)

MARIE:

Your secret is safe with me! Could I write you ever so often... just to see how you are?

KATRINA:

I think I should like that very much. (Nicely) Then I could read YOUR letter here at the nurse's station! But why?

MARIE:

Because I care! We can all use someone to care about us! (Katrina stiffens a bit and then smiles at Marie)

KATRINA:

Goodbye... Auf Wiedersehen... and you WILL write me?

MARIE:

Goodbye. I most certainly will... and thank you.

(BLACKOUT. During the black-out SOUND: Election cheers! Wild radio cheers, parade noises etc. NEWSCASTER'S VOICE: And ladies and gentlemen. PRESIDENT Franklin Delano ROOSEVELT has won the election by an overwhelming 22,809,638 to Herbert Hoover's 15,758,901!!!! The whole country is ecstatic ! FOLKS, let us hope that he follows through on his promises! He promises to take control of our poor economy. He promises us a NEW DEAL! Welcome Franklin and Eleanor Roosevelt. Our country needs you! SONG: "Happy Days are Here Again!"

PARK VOICEOVER:

My sweetie. My 'ittle muse! Finally, it's March 4th! Roosevelt's Inauguration Day! I'm thrilled! The country is thrilled! All of Funnyville is thrilled! The proud citizens have been running all around Funnyville celebrating! It'll be a wonderful thing to have FDR takes the reins of this ol' country! A landslide victory! Maybe he can loan me some of his Hyde Park money! Ha! Ha! Surely now we will get some badly needed relief from these lousy old hard times! The New Deal- it HAS to be better than the OLD Deal! Better yet- Parker Gladden will get some needed relief for himself now that you are finished with your course work! You are NEEDED. Here at home. Here in MY ARMS! I am so proud of you. Kudos to you! My dearest- It has been a long hard haul. Heck... in a teeny while I won't have to miss you more than life! The bus journey will be a short one - especially when you know that I am here waiting for you! And- baby- once you get here, I cannot let you go! Say... baby... that reminds me... how about one baby?... no... maybe two? You are my WORLD!!! LOVE, Park

(SCENE: Barbershop, early morning. Enter Grace)

GRACE:

Hi, there! I just couldn't stay away and I really wanted this place for my business... for our business. I KNOW that we can work out an arrangement that will satisfy us both! (She moves on him!)

PARK:

I've already told you that I am NOT interested in ANY kind of arrangement. MY sink stays in the back! I do not need a phone. The place is just fine and I like it this way!

GRACE:

Well, maybe we can work out a different arrangement... a mutual one. You know what I mean? I find you VERY handsome Parker. I think you and I could get along VERY well.

PARK:

Whoa... young lady!!! Stand your distance! How do I convince you that I am just NOT interested?!! I've tried being polite to you and yet you are so insistent! NOT INTERESTED! I repeat NO, NOT INTERESTED!!! Now, please leave! I am happily in love with a young lady! (He goes to the door and ushers her out) OUT! OUT! I wish you well. LEAVE!!!

GRACE:

(Reluctantly leaving) But. But, we could give it a try. I know how happy I could make you. (He slams door. Once he slams the door, Park breathes deeply. Walks to the mirror. Takes a good look. Smiles. Winks at Marie's photo. Plants a kiss on the photo. Runs his hands through his hair and shakes his head. Park dozes in his chair while WSYR is playing soothing orchestral music. Hottie is seen cruising outside the window with a beer bottle in hand;he is drunk. We see that he wants to go in. He gives a big burp, gestures. (gives the finger?) Hottie leaves. It is early and we see the OPEN sign in the window. We see Marie in the large window. She presses her face against the window and makes faces (a la Park's faces). As she dies this, she gently taps on the door window "Shave and a haircut... 2 bits". Park startles and looks up at window. His smile and excitement increases and he waltzes to the door. Marie and he smile at each other! He picks her up and whirls her around, carrying her inside. SO HAPPY! They embrace. Marie turns the OPEN sign to CLOSED and they smile big! Park smiles and closes the green door window shade. Park sidles to the large window and pulls the green shades. They remain tightly embraced. They dance to the music, kiss, touch each others' faces so lovingly and slowly the curtain rings down.

PARK:

My little Nurtzie... Geepers, I wuv ooooooo! (Slow fade out)

THE END

Letters From Park to his Nurtz

[Marie Hamilton is finishing her time at Crouse-Irving Hospital, Syracuse, NY before she goes off to Brooklyn Hospital where she will be taking advanced courses to be a Pediatrics Charge Nurse. Park Gladden's passion is music ; his instrument, the trombone. Due to his dad's illness, Park becomes the sole bread-winner of the family trying to manage two barber shops. Meanwhile, Park whiles away the lonely hours writing letters to his "Nurtz"and composing music!...Park's barber shop is located just over the "old" bridge on the right as you go up E. Genesee hill.]

September 19,1932
'Marie Dear-

Merely a few lines to let you know that I went yesterday and had a delightful trip. We went to the woods as far as Blue Mountain Lake, then returned via Utica- very nice. Missed YOU, though, and thought how nice it would be had you been along with us. Maybe another time, Yes?

Gee, it's a rather blue old Monday morning- sort of makes me SO lonesome. Have been busy cleaning up the place a bit. Took my dad to Manlius so I am able to be skipper of the ship for now. Yesterday, I took a pledge not to drink all week so I'll have to live up to that! I simply must make go of this shop and that's all there is to that! I've been devilish long enough and I figure it's time to straighten around.

Now, honey- if I understood you correctly over the miserable telephone, you are planning to have Tues. night off OK- I shall call your house late tomorrow to make sure.

Lovingly,
Park...Funnyville, NY

Oct. 13, 1932

Dearest-

Called your mom at 1:30 and told her about the postponement of your holiday, etc. She thanked me very nicely and said that she had planned to meet you for sure.

Oh, gee- just happened to think that I have a date for Friday night- awfully sorry, Marie. It's supposed to be with an RN from Crouse-Irving- gee again- that's right- my error. YOU're the RN at that- I'm so forgetful at times. Right-o- then I'll be seeing you. SMILES!

Howdja like 20,000 in Sing Sing? (I put on the extra zeroes for luck!) Too bad that little boy had to leave at the critical part of the play, wasn't it, mama? Oh, gee- I suppose I'll be spanked Friday night for that! But- lest you forget- I can take it, baby - oh, boy! An' how! There is another concert I'd like to attend at Crouse College but I'm afraid I'm too poor to think about it. Perhaps the next time we're on earth, thing'll be easier- lots of MONEY and whatever! No doubt you'll be attending the ball tonight while I sit at home and bawl. HMMMMM? Are you glistening? Ah, gee- honey- I do get mighty lonesome for you. The time went so quickly Tuesday night I scarcely had time to say "Hello" and then "good-bye".

Oh, by the way - my shoes will have to wait another night for polish. Very inconvenient, don't you think? I'll make them shine Friday night and you'll like it!! Heh, heh, heh! The woim turns. Bee seein ya/

All my love and kisses-

'Night Marie.   LUV- ME

PS Thought you;d look on this side of the paper!. There - an X - just another kiss for you. Feel happier now? Don't cry- Gee- I'll bee seeing you soon- just a few hours. Dry those tears, honey. OOodley- ooday!

October 16, 1932

Darling-

This is one when it hurts to write. I really don't know how to start off or what to say. My actions of yes- terday have spoken in such a way that it would seem nearly impossible to undo them in writing. However- I hereby offer my humble apology in writing in hope that you will consider it and accept it. I'm awfully sorry about it all and whether or not you accept my apology, I swear to never humiliate another woman like that again- whether she be you or someone else. I am trying to do my part by sending these few lines- the rest is quite in your hands now. We have gotten along so perfectly always in every way but one- and -that I assure you is because of my own silliness. So, please give me a bit of consideration- one last time.

Doggie and I have the car torn apart and we hope to have it going again by tomorrow night sometime. If we do, I shall try to come in for a heart-to-heart talk with you tomorrow evening around 8. If we haven't it done, I'll look for words from you concerning Wed. or whatever evening it is that you'll have off.

If I don't hear from you, I'll know that you will not have accepted and you will not forgive me- that is, if you don't see me Tues. night or whenever you have your evening off.. Again- I'm sorry- please believe that.

More love than ever-
Park xxxx ooo

October 18, 1932
My Dearest Marie-

You will see by this letter that I arrived home ok last night so I shan't go into detail about that. Your letter was awaiting me this morning and, indeed, it was interesting. However, I failed to find the portion thereof why you thought I might take offense at, so you must explain on Thurs. night, if you will.

I forgot all about the concert tonight. Had I thought of it last night, I wouldn't have spent my dough for a beer. But, too late now! It's so rainy now I'm afraid that business will be terribly slow today, so I will probably be too poor by night to attend the concert. Guess I shall have to go to bed and dream of it- very well.

This morning I received a card from "Hotdog" (drinking buddy). He said that he was doing quite well in the woods-(don't know in what way but suppose he means with the DEARS!).

It just occured to me that this is an ideal day to shave Mr. Beach (a shut in). If business doesn't come to me -- I can go to it! Clever thought, do you think?

This is certainly what one would term as a blue morning. I just put a shovel of coal on the fire and believe it or not- my coal is blue. Kinsella's "Blue B Coal". How's your uncle?

Gee whiz- come to think of it, I really wanted to borrow a five spot last night and left you in such a hurry that it slipped my mind. I'm so careless that way. Oh well- I won't eat between now and Thursday for spite. I'll bet that'll make you mad. (And I'd bet that it'd make me madder! What do you think?)

There's really no need to carry on further with this silly chatter and as I can't become too serious on such a morning, perhaps I'd best say "cherrio" for now. I shall be expecting to see you Thursday night. Until then- adios!

Toujours l'amour!!

LOVE ...ME!!!!!!

Funnyville, NY November 1, 1932

My Dearest Marie-

Well, here 'tis I- a wee bit sleepy but possibly I can think of a little bit to write this morning. It was exactly 4 when I turned in this morning and could not get to sleep right away. Instead, I snuggled comfortably under the covers and thought of you. Gee- I got to thinking of that tedious bus trip you had just started and and you would get awfully tired before you reached your destination. It's now 10:30 am and I Miss you so much already-don't know what I'll do when Sunday comes. You must have four more hours to go. Gee whiz! Hope you aren't too tired and bored! Tell me about it anyway- won't you, honey?

It has turned out to be a miserable morning and do you think I'm not blue? You have no conception of it yet- haven't had a patron in yet and this sad music playing on the radio just about fills my eyes with grief- here- here- what am I saying? I must say something bright to cheer my little muse. 'Scuse please, but I couldn't help the sentiment.

Well- two hours have lapsed, during which I have earned one dollar and a half. Also have partaken of my noon repast. Now you have only two more hours to go before arriving. Gee, dear- wish I could take your place on that old bus that you may sleep a while in the softest and most comfortable bed in all NY. How'd you like to step into a dance marathon the minute your get off the bus? Oh- dear- I wouldn't believe that you would.

The sun is shining now for a change and my spirits are somewhat lifted. Somewhat- so. But not entirely now. Such will be impossible for some time to come. Gee whiz! Doesn't seem that you've gone- guess I'll go to Crouse Irving tonight- maybe you have not gone at all.- aw - gosh. I'm so nutty- 'scuse please!

Tonight I'm going to retire early. I hope awfully to acquire that good habit regularly now. As I told you- I'm going to do a bit of studying myself! Maybe I can improve my mind- such as it is- poor thing! It's terribly confused right now! "You must study hard and apply yourself, honey. If you don't, you'll regret it one day!" Wish I had done so in music school [Dana School of Music, Youngstown, Ohio] No- Instead I got only half out of it. Of course, I was much younger then but I can see just what I missed. Just blind to opportunity I guess.

After I left you, I breezed along pretty good to Fayetteville. Thought of that old tire blowing out, but I wouldn't mind it a bit knowing that my important mission of seeing you safely aboard the bus was done. I won't have much use for the car now anyway. It was nice during our meetings, though you and know that I shall never ride in it but that I'll think of you

I'll try to shave Mr. Beach and then stop in- as you suggested - to say "hello" to your mom.

This noon for dinner I ate some of that bunny that Fetteroff gave me yesterday. So- no doubt I'll be leaping and bounding all over town shortly.

I hope your squirrel effects weren't displayed too badly. No doubt you were scrambling about the bus alot. But then, you must have needed the exercise. Yes? No? By the way, I hope those tough lookin' mugs didn't start a gang war in the bus? And did the sailor have a wife in every port? I must post this letter right away so that you may receive it real soon. So- I will say "CHERRIO" for now. Don't forget I am missing you, sweetheart. Must be love, hmmmmmm? Are you listening? 'TIS!

Love and kisses-

Park

Good luck, honey- success to you!

Sat. Nov. 2, 1932

My Dearest Marie-

Your big fat and long and sweet letter and interesting letter came this morning and I nearly devoured it. Saturday... It's a long hard day anyway and I feel inspired after reading such a sweet letter.

Yesterday afternoon, I became busy at 4 straight til past 9- didn't even have time to eat. I was so tired that I drove to Manlius and ordered 4 bottles of Janack's beer. I thought of the time we were there and got real blue. I didn't stay as long as I was in bed by 11:30! BOY! O BOY! Since you've been gone, I surely am blue! I'll miss going to the old annex for you tomorrow, too - It's a terrible old feeling- the loneliness- isn't it, honey? Here's the tune but, please do not attempt to play or sing it in public! Rather silly, but then I had to get it out of my system. If I could write words as readily as I write music, I'd send lots of songs But, dammmit- the words don''t come out!

Your beloved brother, Charles, stopped in yesterday and gave me another shot of that TNT (Homemade Hooch!) that he had the other night. Didn't taste so good this time, so I went easy with it. He was asking me what news I had from you but I only told him that all was well. One can't tell EVERYTHING- you know! (SMILES!)

This powerful Katrina who rules you must be an immense woman. Guess maybe you had better obey her wishes- what do you think? She sounds like something from a Wagnerian opera!

The sun has been shining brightly this afternoon for a change. It has been rainy ever since you left!

Awfully sorry that you have that cold and be sure to take care of yourself. Gee whiz- I don't want my 'ittle nurse to get sick. I suppose such a ride on a bus would make anyone sick... though.

That was funny about the hat that you saw. Talk about dreams coming true- guess you know how to have them come true alright. I WILL have a different hat when we meet again- won't that be lovely? I have to keep my eye on this old brown one- mom has threatened to burn it many times!

Gee, honey, I must cut this rather short as I expect to be busy soon. Be a good girl, dear- and write lots of letters. Guess I'll have to drive to Nasshos and look at our pig again tomorrow.

All my LOVE- ever thinking of you-

Park xxxxxxxxxxxxxxxxxxxxxxxxooooooooooooooooooooooooo

Nov. 4, 1932

Dearest Marie-

It's time my dear Mademoiselle Hamilton - thought that I answered that lovely letter I received yesterday morning. Here goes- I would have written yesterday but I seem to be possessed by a peculiar mood and I didn't feel like writing. Maybe it was one of those hateful, ugly days. I don't know. I never feel the same from day to day. Wish my disposition were smooth and even like yours but I guess I wasn't cut out that way. Sorry.

Last night, it became snowy about 9 P.M. and was miserably cold throughout the night. Talk about need- ing an Armstrong heater! I certainly need one- the M.H. brand-preferably. Perhaps in another month such will happen, huh? Anyway, you know I hope so.Three weeks have gone by already- only about 4 more!

Sat. night I was exceptionally good for a change! Dog and I had a LITTLE wine (and I mean little) then went over to Manlius Center just as the dance was ending. It was an uneventful evening but safe and sane- that much I know. Sunda, Dog and I got busy and fixed the ceiling part of my car. We had to chase to E. Syracuse and look around for spare parts. Consequently, my car is running "pip" again.

Sunday pm, I really did take a nap and didn't get up to shave Mr. Beach at all. I guess he is really low- if Harold comes 'round, I'll ask him if it's ok to shave his dad now. If he is out of his mind, though- he probably doesn't mind the whiskers so much. Poor fellow- It must be awful to suffer so long- just to die by inches. Bad enough to think about that, isn't it?

Sunday we had a little theatre party- I was merely the chauffeur, though, and that's not saying much. My mom and dad, Bill Hawkins and wife and I went to Syracuse and into the early show at Eckel [movie theater]. We saw "Air Mail". It was good- in fact, the whole show was excellent! We left F'ville at 6:30 and were home around 10. I listened to the radio til 11 and then turned in for the night. Another safe, sane night.

Only a few days 'til Thanksgiving. What am I going to do? I don't know, but it'll still be safe and sane what- ever I do. Now, isn't that nice?? What have I to be thankful for? O woe! Here you are away from me- I'm not happy about it. Dammit! No. I wish you were here so that we might do something exciting- and- do you think it would be exciting? Ah baybee- ah, hell. What's the use- we'll just have to patiently wait for another time. Sad But true- isn't it, honey?

By the way, I suppose I must drive up to Pulaski one day soon and visit your friend, Ann. poor girl- must be lonesome. But then, she couldn't be more lonesome than I. Don't worry though- I think I'll change my mind and stay right here in Funnyville and wait for you. Too cold up in Pulaski country to suit me!

Well- little buttercup- I had better post this now or you won't receive it soon enough!

All my love for you-

Park. PS Be good, dammmmmmmit!!

November 7, 1932

Marie Dearest-

Perhaps my letters are coming too frequently. I don't want to annoy you TOO much! But, gee whiz-it's a quiet afternoon and as I am thinking of you, I may as well let you know about it.

Saturday night I was real good for change. Went up to Eastman's at about 11:30 (all alone) and had only one pitcher of beer which wasn't good at all. Then I drove over to Manlius Center and watched them dance in that marathon until 1 am. A quiet, uneventful evening but I felt good and arose early for Sunday morning. Wasn't that nice?

Shaved Mr. Beach around 1:30 Sunday afternoon. No one was there when I went to the door but Rose came over and admitted me. Charles had to come over after I got to work which rather spoiled things-Ha. Ha. Don't take me seriously now. Afterward I stopped in at your house- they were having their Sunday repast. Your mom told me that she heard from you and I told her SOME of the contents of your letter! I was invited to eat but I had already promised to be home for dinner at 2. I had to decline. They all looked the same but- gosh- with you away, the interest just wasn't!

At 3 pm I turned on the radio and listened to the symphony concert. Lazed on the davenport and fell asleep- slept 'til 4:30 and missed the entire concert! Did I ever sleep! Boy, o Boy! At 8 pm, my dad and I drove to town and went to the Strand (Syracuse movie theater) where we saw "Goona Goona"- a South Sea Isle Picture with a cast of natives. Also- "Virtue" with Carole Lombard ad Pat O'Brian. "Virtue" was very interesting- I liked it loads. Oh, yes...It was an exact duplicate of the night we went to the Strand- rained like hell when we went in and rained like hell when we came out! But after I got home, I didn't roll on the dining room floor. I would be silly to roll alone,wouldn't it? I'll have to be with my "holy roller" in order to make it exciting.

Business has been quite good today. Suppose everyone is getting fixed up for the big election.

Gee, I missed seeing you yesterday afternoon! I forgot to tell you that I went to Manlius at 5 (just as it got dark) and drove up our old road to the tracks. Guess the car went where it wanted to go of its own accord. Anyway- I walked all around where we did that one Sunday but I got so lonesome I couldn't stand it any longer. Just thought I'd go there once more before the snow fell. (That's that! Shows that I'm thinking of you anyway, Doesn't it?)

My Aunt Grace and her new husband, Bill, arrived here Saturday and yesterday morning. They left for Newark- taking my grand-dad with them. He intends to stay a month. Poor old fellow had his things packed and ready two days before they came for him. He gets pretty lonesome now that his gardening days are over.

Noticed this picture in the paper and thought you might be interested. Is this the baby who used to disturb our gentler conversation when I'd come up nights? And will mail this.

Well, dearest- I must go for now. Home to grab a bite to eat. Will mail this and inquire for mail at the post office.

Your hospital view card came this a.m. Looks very nice!

Beee good and I AM being good, don't forget that!

Love and kisses-

Park

Nov. 9, 1932

Dearest Marie-

Received a nice letter from you this a.m and- gee whiz- Each letter becomes nicer- what am I going to do about it? Cry? Laugh? Well- I nearly do both- gee- I miss you so at times- maybe I don't exactly cry, but there are times when my eyes are filled with tears! Why is it? Ah, dammit! About 6 weeks yet and I'll be seeing you.Well, I'll wait and be good, too!

We had a card from my dad written on Saturday last. He was in Alexandria, Virginia. He said there was about 10 inches of snow at the time there. Not very encouraging there! No doubt by now he's about in Florida where there won't be any snow. I only hope he starts feeling better- gee- he looked real bad when he left- I was worried.

I'm going well at the barber shop but I have to go like hell to keep up the rents, etc. ,(His dad's barbershop is in Manlius) Guess I'll have to put my car up after this week. I have Mason's dues, musician's union dues, etc. to pay. I figure they come before a car license. Besides the car (if it holds together) will come in handier in the spring- especially on certain nights. What do you think? Well, I'll wait to see about that, too!

It's now Thursday a..m. Got busy last night and had to lay over 'til now. Sorry. You spoke of a New Year's resolution. Well- sweetheart- I intend to make quite a few. Gee, I only hope I can live up to them. Wish I could cut out the old booze entirely. Anyway,I intend to try no matter how hard this can be.

We received a card from dad this a.m. from St. Petersburg, Fl. He said he still wasn't feeling well yet. Only hope that he improves real soon- makes me depressed as the deuce to have him down there and ill. The trip down was strenuous enough for a well person- perhaps when he is more permanently settled he WILL feel better.

Your brother dropped in a minute ago- he was driving Roger's truck as Klock is ill- says the job would last him 2 or 3 days longer.

Gee- sweetheart- I miss you so! I know I'd feel more like working if I knew I was to see you this night. Suppose I can weather it 'til February- can hardly wait 'til February comes- how about that?

Yesterday your mom, Dot and Lillian passed by- I was busy but happened to look thru the window just at the right time to throw them a "hello!"

Well- honey- I can't think of anymore to speak of, so I'll close for now. Hope you are feeling your old self by this time. Hate to think if YOU were not well also.

All my love always-

Park xxxxooooooo All my kissess just for you- the moustache is gone but I'll sow another one when you come home to me. XXX

November 10, 1932

My Dearest Marie-

Thus far a.m. things are going so slow so I shall attempt a few lines... If you don't mind. Your letter came yesterday and I fairly ate it up- dandy honey. I'm so glad when I hear from you.

You have been gone one week now. So far, the time passed quickly although I've missed you like the devil. Don't mean that exactly - couldn't miss the devil so much but I have really missed you. You just bet I have, honey!

"Hot Dog" dropped in town yesterday a.m to vote. He said he likes it back in the woods and left again yesterday afternoon. Guess he'll be back here for good in about 3 weeks. He said he'll fix up what's left of my car then. Oh yes- made another payment on the thing Monday, so possibly I'll have it when you return after all. (If it doesn't fall apart due to old age by then!)

Yes, I have been exceptionally good since you left. I think so anyway. If I can only keep up the good work I'll be ok. I must keep trying, I suppose. Gee- whiz- glad I'm trying to do something worthwhile or a change. I guess I've been running wild long enough and it's time for an awakening long of some sort.

I was awfully sorry to learn that you aren't feeling quite yourself, honey. I suppose that things might be worse though under certain conditions. Maybe you think that I'm glad that they're not though- for your sake, at least. The word is in need of bigger and better people- no doubt of that- but I suppose those things can wait. Right O?

If you can't make it home for Christmas time, perhaps I can come there. Every other Saturday night I notice they have excursions to NYC via the Lackawana RR for $4.50 round trip. The train leaves Syracuse at about 1:00 Saturday night arriving in NYC about 6 am. Leaves for Syracuse again sometime Sunday night. But it would give us a few hours together anyway. Don't worry- we'll make some plans to be together- even if it's for a short while. Think I'm not anxious? - gee whiz- let's not be silly!

I thought Fayetteville would be lively yesterday- but on the contrary. Well, let's hope things will shape up after Roosevelt takes the wheel although it seems that the good times would be held up that much longer. It'll be tough old pickings, I'm afraid. My business was slow Monday but yesterday was terribly slow.

I missed seeing "Red Dust" when it played here but when it returns again, I shall surely see it. Gee-you're so lucky in a way- there are so many nice things in the amusement area to see in NYC. If I were there, I'd no doubt spend all my money on theatres, operas, etc.

By the enclosed, you can readily see what my dear sister (Geniveve) thinks of me. Ain't a dandy? I'll get even with her, though. Just wait and see! The very idea- I could smash her!

Well, little sweetheart- I can't think of anything new that would interest you right now- so I will say- So Long and good luck 'til the next time!

Beaucoup d'amour and plenty of kisses-

Park xxxxxxxxxxx0000000000000

P.S. Good night, Marie- be seeing you Sunday afternoon- really early. (Sounds good?) Wish it could be!

Nov. 12, 1932 Thurs. a.m

My Dearest Sweetheart-

Just now opened for business and your letter arrived. It was a real nice one, too. Honey- Thanks so much. Had to write this morning not only to answer your letter but to enclose the ad my sister sent. Anyway- I hope I remember to put it in this envelope. 'Scuse please- awfully sorry. I noticed when returning from the Post office yesterday p.m. I had forgotten to enclose that ad!

Looks like the "big horse" (Katrina, Head Nurse) sort of cares for you, honey! Guess we can never judge another by size. Look at an elephant- not nearly as harmful as certain little bugs! Gee- honey- I'm bugs about YOU! Shut up!

Last night my dad came home at about 8 o'clock and asked me to accompany him to the Regent (movie theater) to see "Life begins". As I had already seen that show (with you),I told him that I'd go to another theater and pick him up afterwards. So, I went to Loews, and to my amazement "Red Dust" was still on there. I thought it had left. So, I went in and enjoyed it very much.- a real good story, I thought. Gee. Guess it gave me about the same sensation that you experienced. Kind of a queer old feeling, don't you think??

What a gloomy old morning it is out! Raining and also dark- wish I could have remained 'neath the quilts a bit longer. Tough- I HAVE to get up in the mornings.

Well, I haven't heard from Miss Ohio (sister Gen) yet nor have I written her. I figure I've souped around long enough and life's too short to worry over such things- especially when so much time has been spent in trying.

My old big left toe has been sore again since yesterday. So this morning I put some of your zinc oxide from the little tin box on it. Then bandaged it. Can't figure out why the soreness returns every once in a while. Wish you had been here to bandage it up for me- I know then I would be healed well real soon. Anyway, it did one time when you fixed it.

I do not know many pounds I've lost since you left but I'll admit I get damned lonesome at times. You and I always got along pretty nice together, didn't we? And when we didn't, it was my fault or rather the fault of wine. But don't worry, we'll have some nicer times, somehow, somewhere, sometime.

Well, I must mail this and take some nourishment!

Don't forget- I'm being real good and you do the same. Watch out for those professional men the fortune teller spoke of. Guess I'll have to slay a doctor or two yet!

Loads of love and kisses-

Park xxxxxooooooooo

Nov. 13, 1932

My Dearest Mickey-

The mailman just came- rather expected a little letter this morning. A bit disappointed but perhaps one will arrive as I shall go to the post office late this p.m. and ask.

Haven't been doing anything exciting since I saw Loew's the other night. Thursday night I retired about 11 and last night I was in bed by midnight. Looks like I am reformed.. Doesn't it?

Thursday night- a chicken supper was featured at the Methodist Church so I thought I'd go and help the good old Methodists along a bit. At 6:30, closed for a half hour and went up. It was the first time I've been in a church building in many months and I felt uneasy! Saw your mom, Dot, Roy, Rose and Charles there. Didn't notice them until after I ate, so I went over to say "hello". Looked like a family picnic- if you had been there, I guess we could term it one. Anyway, the feed was good and I enjoyed myself.

Last night, Lee Giles (however you spell i!) was in for a scrape. And he said to send you his regards. Heasked about you! And looks about the same. His head is practically healed now.

Well, tomorrow is another Sunday and I suppose it'll be a lonely one for me. It'll try to listen to the symphony again- maybe I can keep awake once. These days are so dark and gloomy that I get awfully sleepy at times. I figure when I'm asleep, I keep out of mischief, So- that's something, isn't it? You have been gone nearly two weeks now so it's nearer to Christmas now than it was. Won't be long- I guess. Gee, honey - I miss you so much on Thursday nights. Seems like I should be going to your home after I close the place. You have been gone nearly two weeks now so. It's nearer to Christmas than it was. Won't be too long, I guess.

Probably I'll shave Mr. Beach again tomorrow. Makes it easier to shave him once a week. I'll drop by and say hello to your solks- I mean you folks! Here comes business so I must work. Will write more after. Heaps of love and kisses,

Park

P.S. this is a rather cold letter but I'll be warmer next time. Maybe it's because the shop is so cold!

Nov. 15, 1932

My Dearest Mickey-

Just received your two letters written Sunday, and I am certainly glad to hear from you, honey. It's been two weeks this a.m. since I helped you move from the Crouse-Irving annex- 14 long days, dammit! When I think back- it seems like an age! Don't think it's silly when you try to imagine those times. Many times I sit here doing nothing and I catch myself picturing in my mind nearly everything we USED to do. Our trips to Eastwood- Nash's pigs...O gee! What's the use? Maybe it's silly but it is SO pleasant to think about anyway, isn't it sweetheart? Memories mean alot to me and always will.

I don't believe that you have any reason at all to let Miss Ohio worry you! It's over 2 months since I heard from her last and it looks as if we're all caught up. What do you think? Yes, and dammit! The violinist who used to play with me in that Ohio Theatre Orchestra had the same name as that med student and was a bad one for the young women! This violinist had two or three brothers- maybe he's related to the student!. This young med student has me worried! Tosti? Must be an Italian! You might ask him if he ever lived in Warren, Ohio or has relatives there.

Gee- honey girl- Saturday night I slipped off the wagon- unintentionally. You see, I went to Manlius and got my dad after work and came home with him. My mother and Grace were out somewhere and I guess it was about 11 pm. Well- I thought I'd go to Manlius Center and watch them dance once again. But first I decided to go over to that speakeasy directly behind our house for a bit "tuning up". Gee- he had some of the darndest gin That I ever tasted. At first I got a ½ pint- sat there and consumed it. Then -not being satisfied, I ordered another ½ pint. Well- the time sped on and it was after 1:00. I knew the dance would be over and I suppose I had another Little one after that. Then, the first thing I knew- I didn't know much of anything! Guess I got into my car and drove right home (only half a block!). I got into the house and Grace and mom were sleeping in a new bed mom just got. Well- I had to wake them up and I couldn't be coaxed into going to bed. Mom's temper got the best of her and she beat me with the broom. I don't remember that part. She had to get my poor dad into this and I guess we clinched and wrestled. I know he had me by the neck once and I broke the hold by pressing my elbow into his chest. We battled for a while. MY own ills are about over but I ache all over and am bruised! My neck has a deep scratch about 4 inches long in the back. It must have been a terrible fight. I think I broke one of dad's chest bones.Gee, that's what hurts most of all. He hasn't been feeling well- wish I had received the worse end of this. I deserved it. That damned booze anyway! I hope I've had enough! If mom had used her head I would have gone to bed quietly but she's so excitable! Dammit...I'm ashamed of myself- keep this to yourself now- don't let anyone know what an ass I am! Just don't know when I've had enough of the stuff! I should not taste another bit again...not even a little. THIS IS THE LAST- I HOPE! You don't know how sorry I am.That's the first I've done anything since you left. Haven't seen any girls at all since you left - and won't until you return. And then- well- use your judgment. I miss you so much and can hardly wait till we meet again. It's a wonder why you haven't left me flat the way I drink and all before seeing you. Your patience must be good or else you must care for me a lot. I am so sorry about everything and I realize it's up to me to pull myself back up. This I shall try to do, believe me.

Sunday, I dozed around the house and went to bed at 6 P.M. I slept til 7:45 Monday a.m. Guess the long sleep helped heal my bruised body! "A Sweetheart is Forever" just came on the radio- WSYR. And does that ever make me sad! So many tunes remind me of you- gee- especially when I'm sitting here alone. A woosy old feeling. Do you notice I'm catching all these "gees" from you? You've no doubt caught the "gee, whizzes" from me by now. And that makes us even. Did I say "even" honey? No. C'est impossible! I can never even things up with you. I've been too bad. And you're always nice to me about everything. Anyway, little sweetheart - don't worry about my being good. About women- I mean! I slipped the other day the other way and I'm sorry I'm saving all my love for you! You watch out for those professional men! Remember the fortune teller!

All my Love (real, too!)

Park

Dearest-

Nov. 16, 1932

Read your letter just now- the one telling of you trip downtown. Bet it was quite a treat for you. I certainly wish I might have been with you Saturday and Sunday nights. I'm sure we would have a great time together. Perhaps I can make the Lackawanna excursion some time on a Sunday. Then we most certainly would enjoy ourselves, think not?

Yesterday going to work, my dad went up to the doctor's and he discovered that his sternum was broken! Doc strapped it up and I guess that feels better. Wish it had been my head instead! Guess maybe it would have been better all around then. That damned booze- wish they had never discovered how to make it. Because of Prohibition there are no rules- who knows what crap we are getting? My dad told Doc that we were fooling around, so never mention the real incident to anyone, will you? He had a terrible strangle-hold on me- I had to get free one way or another. Accidents will happen- I am so terribly sorry and such a thing will NEVER happen again. If it could have been someone other than my own dad I wouldn't care so much. There are alot of birds I'd like to crush- but It might prove disastrous. He now coughs so much that I know it must hurt him. I'll remember not to squeeze YOU too hard when we next meet!

Saw brother- Charles -on the street yesterday and he was telling me about the letter in which you sent me your love! I asked him if he expected to send your hate- I guess that's fixed. He'll be ok when he has lived a while longer!

There is something fascinating about those subways, isn't there? Guess it was 1925 when I first tried them. I rode them so much that after I returned home, I imagined that I could still hear them rattle and rumble.

Monday night my dad and I went to Syracuse. He went to the Eckel and I took in Keith's where I saw "I Am A Fugitive" featuring Paul Muni. Gee! It was thrilling! I don't believe I would ever care to become a chain gang member after seeing that picture. A terrible thing!

Speaking of Armstrong heaters, hmm ...think I'm not missing mine? This is the season when one needs one most but I believe I can wait for a wee while. In fact, I intend to wait! If one can wait 2 weeks, I believe I can wait much longer. It'll only be 4 days more anyway- and what's that- a mere drop in the bucket.The main thing I find is to keep one's mind occupied- time goes faster. What do you think?

It has been beautiful out for the last 2 weeks. I believe I can wait a tad longer. If I had the afternoon off, I'd like to take a long walk somewhere. Wouldn't it be nice to be alone, though- much nicer if you could be along. Due to my bruises, I didn't get to shave Mr. Beech Sunday but shall go THIS Sunday at the latest. Perhaps I'll know enough to retire early this Saturday night instead of trying to change my natural disposition.

Here's business so must close for now!

Love and kisses-

Park xxxxxoooooo Must be love..'TIS!

Nov. 18, 1932

My Dearest Marie-

I shall attempt writing at home for change so you must excuse the ink. All right-if you don't want to excuse it! Shut up! Trying to change my natural disposition. No- really- I don't feel quite that badly but to tell you the truth, I'm awfully tired. You don't have to run and tell the head of the hospital! Just plain tired! The hospital might not be interested!

MY! What a start off! Now, what are you thinking? No doubt you're saying,"He's drunk again!"but my dear young lady, I'm not. Not with alcohol, anyway. Just intoxicated by my HARD day's work. Wot a laff! - I'm serious- really... Fayetteville and my hard work are killing me by the inches. I came home with my dad about 9:15 tonight so you can see I'm trying to be a good little lad. *Even strummed for 45 minutes on the piano previous to this writing- yes- even sang 3 or 5 songs all by my lonesome! They made me think of you- there, now isn't that something? Don't cry- Marie- gee whiz, don't cry!*

My dad says his sternum is feeling a trifle better. No doubt he'll be sore for another 2 weeks or so- poor fellow. Honestly- I feel like I had murdered him. It's the first thing I think of when I awake in the morning - had such a serious neck-hold on me. It hurts me as if someone was running a knife through me. In a way though, it wasn't all my fault- gee, he would have choked me to death. That wouldn't have been too pleasant either! Guess I was intoxicated alright-think I wasn't? But, it shan't ever happen again. NEVER! Not worth it!

I haven't seen any of your folks lately- saw your mom last - let's see- a week ago Thursday night. There- fore, I didn't know Mr. Beach was sinking so low. However, I shall go by there with my tools and shave him- if he's too ill, I can at least find out what's what. Probably I'll stop at your house for a while although I feel bluer yet while I enter therein. I don't know- the place isn't the same without you. My 'ittle nurse - do I miss you?? Just ask me.

You're not the only one who looks over a memo book. Nearly every day I glance through mine and dream of the pleasant hours that we spend together! Most pleasant hours we passed together!

Yes! I remember the night we went with Harold and his girl- gee whiz! Thought we'd never be able to evade them! Seems like only yesterday! The whole summer sped by too fast to suit me. Seems like a wonderful dream, doesn't it? The times we went to Greene's and all - gosh- wish it were just about to happen all over again. I'm awfully sorry about those "mean" spells I had. Guess I didn't really mean them to be- just funny old moods took over!

And July 4th night! It's a wonder you didn't give me the old "gate" right then. I guess I deserved it though. Anyway-I am awfully glad you didn't- why? Aw gee! I cannot explain it- just a funny old feeling around my heart. Think you'll ever fall in love, Marie? Don't do it-

Gee- it's awful- very sad. I know my old heart misses you, honey. It's just plain lonesome! 'Scuse please- it's late and I must get plenty of sleep tonight. Hope I dream pleasant dreams of you, my dear. I dream of you all the day but the dreams of sleep are lovelier - don't you think so?

Good night, Marie. See you early. Oh, I forgot you asked me not to say it all again.

All my love for you-

Park xxxxxooooooooo P.S. You be good, darn ya!

Dec. 3, 1932

Dearest Marie-

Another letter came from Brooklyn this a.m. so I'll answer it right away 'ere II get busy. You said nothing about being sick or shall I say, sicker. Anyway- I'm glad of that- gee whiz- don't want YOU sick again.

I have refused to sleep out with Hotty a couple of times and I think he's a bit sore about it. I'm staying home nights all this week trying to take care of myself as much as possible. Haven't even run my car and I guess that part will be done after Saturday night. Guess they expect to have a blowout at the house Saturday, but I'm going to take your advice and not drink after 12 midnight! Really, I'm going to settle down- more business less pleasure.- but is it? Anyway- false pleasure and the real thing are quite different, aren't they?

Well, sweetheart- I shall call your mom this p.m. and ask regarding you. Keep a stiff upper lip, backbone, etc. Honey- We'll be together again before long. I'll write real often.

All my love for you,

Park

December 6, 1932

Dearest Marie-

Meant to write yesterday but didn't get to it for one reason or another. But YOUR long, sweet letter came yesterday. Gee- it must be tough to have to remain abed for so long. I'm sorry I can't call you to try to cheer you up a bit. That menu scheme didn't look too appetizing to be sure but no doubt the best under these certain Circumstances.

Saturday night my dad was the sickest he's been yet. Could scarcely get his breath. We had to call Doc Sam and he told him he must stay in bed for several days- along with this and the medicine he prescribed complete bed rest.- dad is feeling 100% better although he still is weak and unable to go to work. The doc told me that he would have contracted pneumonia had he not taken care of himself immediately. He was so run down- no resistance whatsoever.

Sunday evening I stopped and talked with your mom. She read your letter to me which was interesting enough - but- dammit. I hated to think of you lying there in bed as you wrote it. Well- anyway- keep up the old spunk and no doubt we'll see each other before too long. I know I' m anxious about it- how about you? Sunday evening before going to your house I was trying to carve off leg of lamb and cut my forefinger instead. Gave it a dirty cut- in fact, it didn't stop bleeding so I drove up to Doc Sam's and he bandaged it for me. It seems to be healing pretty good now although I'm afraid of infection whenever anything like that happens.

We had my grand dad down while for Sunday dinner. He seems to keep in good health. Had a good time in Newark but said he was glad to get back to his little house again. After Sunday dinner, I played piano as he tried to sing some of his English songs but the old fellow couldn't sing worth trying. My grandma and he used to sing these songs together whenever we had them at the house, so I guess he got to thinking of her Sunday. Gee- it was pathetic- too much for me.

Well, sweetheart - it's dinner time so I'll mail this on my way home. Now don't take your illness too seriously - just think- I am always thinking of you and it won't be long before we can be together again.

All my love-
Park

Dec. 10, 1932
My Dearest Marie-
I just now called your mom to inquire of your condition and she said that you were gradually im- proving since the terrible night you put in Sunday. Gee-honey- I'm so sorry. It must have been an awful night. Anyway- I'm glad that you're coming along good now. Don't worry about things here- everything's ok- just take good care of yourself when you're out of bed- build up your strength before trying to venture home. I am very anxious to see you but- gee whiz- I'm concerned about your health as well.

It has turned real cold these last couple of days. In fact, it has put a real crimp in business. Yesterday afternoon,it snowed so hard and I saw a couple cars turn completely around when they skidded on E. Genesee St. hill. It's risky business driving in the winter. I'll feel after when my old car is up or the winter, especially when I have no insurance!

they are going to hustle, or rather, play out the contestants by making them do laps in a given time. The thing is lasting so long that the management is getting worried. None of that for me- how about you? For $100,000 I might try- no more - no less!

Dammit - I've looked everywhere for that money order but to no avail. I must have dropped it on the post office floor when I got your letter. And now i must wait a month for the authorities to trace it. Some days you just can't save a nickel. Just some more of life, I suppose.

Have been busy now. It is now 6 p..m. and I just went to the post office and got your letter. What a letter! Have been busy now. I'm so glad that you are getting along so well- boy- am I not glad! Don't you dare try to over-do it now or I'll thrash you when you get home. Just take things easy, won't you?

Yes- my dear- keep out of the cemeteries! Gee- that paper didn't leave much to the imagination, did it? Anyway- I'll stick to the spot over the tracks- won't be too bad to state in court. Homewood should have taken her into the woods and then upset a canoe or something.

YOU are awfully damned sweet - my dearest. Perhaps I'm falling in love with you! Don't ever fall in love, will you? Boy- it's awfully painful. NEVER FALL!

I don't recall that your mom read the mushy parts of your letter or not. I was rather nervous as I was concerned whether you were alive or not!

It's been 2 weeks since Stanton was hurt- he's coming along well as can be expected. No doubt he'll .be in for 3 weeks more. Guess his heart has moved about 1 ½ inches! They're afraid to move him on account of his collar bone- afraid it will slip out of place. I'm going to shave him this afternoon- last time was Tues. night. He'll have a good crop tomorrow- heavy whiskers, anyhow.

It's nearly 6:30 so I'll close and mail this and maybe go out tonight.

Don't forget, I'm always thinking of you- can hardly wait until you come home. And do you think I don't love you tremendously!!!!

All My LOVE-
Park xxxooo

Dec. 13, 1932
My Dearest Marie-

Didn't exactly feel in a writing mood yesterday but maybe this a.m. I can do better!

Sunday afternoon a Syracuse hairdresser came to the house and inquired about using the rear of the barber shop as a hair-dressing parlor. She wanted to give me 25% of what she took in- I'd have to install a phone, have gas piped in, etc. I'm to call her this a.m. and let her know my decision. I'll tell her she must pay $15 a week if she wants the place.I don't like the percentage idea at all. With her way of doing things, she may move out in a week or two leaving me with the phone etc. on MY hands. A tad too soft for her, methinks.

Believe it or not, I haven't tasted alcohol since last Thurs. night. I've gone to bed at about 11 o'clock and feel much better for doing so. My folks are so surprised that they don't know how to take it. To tell the truth, I was getting to the point where I felt so puck I had to reform. With my dad sick and all, I can't afford to be taken sick, too. My dad went to the Manlius shop and tried to work yesterday but he feels so wobbly and weak. He has a chance to go to Florida around New year's with a fella room Cazenovia. I think it would do him good but I don't know whether he'll accept the offer or not.

Gee, I hope you're gradually becoming your old self again. Just think- only 12 days more til Christmas. All the presents I desire - my dear- is YOUR presence. Quite enough for me- can hardly wait to see you again. It has been 1 1/2 months since you left- a LONG time, sweetheart. But the next few months will pass by swiftly and - then- well- we'll see. Think not?

Sunday night, mom, dad and I drove in and went to the Eckel. Clive Brook in "Sherlock Holmes". It was a milder version of the story but proved interesting- nonetheless. Prior to the show, I hadn't been in quite a while so this was a treat!

My old car runs good yet and no doubt I'll still be driving at Christmas time..probably til the 1st anyway. Then I'll store it away til after winter. Possibly one night while you're here, we'll have a balmy summer night- I'll place an order for one anyway- wouldn't that be nice?

Must go to lunch so will say goodbye for now.

All my love-

Park xxxxoooo

Dec. 17, 1932

MY Dearest Marie-

How's the little girl today? Lots better, I hope. Wish it could be that i could say "hello" in person but it won't be long until I shall be able to do so, will it? Old time is flying- -only 8 more days til Christmas.

By the way, I didn't accidently place my money order made out to Oneida Bank in the envelope of yesterday's letter, did I? In the am when I first came on the job, I brought the money order and two envelopes. The bank said that enclosed in their envelope was a letter and the note, but no money order. It just occurred to me that I might have paced the money order in the second envelope...to you. Take a look, anyway, honey. Your mom said it was hard for you to procure stationery so I'm going to enclose some for you. I realize that everything must be in your dorm room, hard to get at it and YOU are stuck in the hospital bed!

My dad is feeling somewhat better now. This a.m. he got dressed and came here to the shop. I cut his hair and shaved him. He looks bad, though, it's pitiful. He sort of tottles when he walks. I advised him to go back home to rest some more. Wish I could do more for him but there's nothing more I CAN do, it seems. He hasn't been able to work since last Friday- perhaps he will have to give up the Manlius shop as I believe it is too much for him at the present.

Brother Charles came around yesterday and we visited for a while. He gets depressed, I imagine, having no job.Like so many others during these times. Times are really tough. This town seems to be getting more quiet every day. It's a fright.. .I know I can't afford to do much these days. I'm going to keep my car going (if possible) til the first of the year- then store it somewhere till spring. I don't really need it now. It'll be nicer in the spring, do you think? Especially when you are here to ride in it. Gee - I look forward to the time!

Well- honey girl- I must get to work so will close for now

All my love,

Park Hope you are feeling loads better. I'm ALWAYS thinking of you.

Dec. 19, 1933

Sweetheart-

Perhaps it's silly of me to write - I meant only to surprise you and then again, perhaps you will have more ambition with which to go about your duties on Tuesday.

Business started off much better today than it did a week ago. It had been a beautiful day- the main reason for it no doubt.

Mr. Newton of the Newton Motor Car Co. of Chittenango just dropped in a gave me a note that I might proceed with payments on my car. I'm going to pay 50 cents this time- that'll only make a $35 balance - not so bad.

My mother hadn't returned by noon so my dad and I had salmon and potatoes for lunch. This may sound a bit fishy- but it's the truth nonetheless.

Last night I went immediately to bed and I don't believe I ever slept more soundly. My dad called me a half dozen times this a.m. Guess it was the 6th call that I heard him. After lunch today, I flopped on my daybed and slept another hour! Better give me some medicine of something tomorrow night- need a tonic -

I guess. One minus alcohol though- Now, isn't that nice?

Life- my dear- is so satisfying, isn't? Death is more of a mystery still. And-Love? ...well love is so like inflating a rubber balloon - it starts out so flat - and grows- and grows- blows. Gets bigger and fatter yet, yes - often it bursts-- but sometimes it expands to great proportions, reaching - it seems to the ends of the earth. It's nice - though- n'est-ce pas? Fascinating- ever new - thrilling. At least it should be that way. I- for one, should hate it to be otherwise-shouldn't you? Oh,well- I shan't think further on such a big subject- we're all too ignorant- all of us- to try to understand and appreciate such a subject

By the way, How'd you like to be slapped down by a huge Ontario wave right now? Wouldn't it be sad, though? Wny- honey- do you think I'd let such an angry lake hurt you? NO SIR! I'd smash it right back so hard- oh, gee! My right leg is so sore today- you, you- gee, Still from when you pinched me so hard that night. Oh, well you're the only one who will pinch me but you've got one coming. Don't forget that! An extremely cruel girl, honey- can't understand why you should desire to treat such a gentle soul as I so cruelly. Another mystery- a mystery that I shall never solve, but then, why try? I love those pinches but not such severe ones.

Love YOUUUUUU-

Park xxxooo

Dec. 20, 1932

Dearest-

Hope I shall still have my car and also I hope that I can afford to license it by the time you get here. If not- I guess I'll have to have fireside dates with you and maybe soon you'll get fed up with them and then give me the "gate" or something of the kind. It's hell to be poo, honey, but we have lots of fun for poor people, don't We? We doost!

Hotty stuck around until I closed the shop but I got through just in time to catch the 8:05 bus to Manlius And left him standing in front of the shop. I had to go up for a haircut- either that or get a violin and THEY come at a rather high price in these hard times!

Well- sweetheart- work had and study hard and do not forget that I wait patiently for the day when we shall meet again!

All my love-

Park   Mima rakastan Sinnas- Maybe some of the Finnish nurses can translate this for you - HA.

Just 3 little words. Cheerio- Good Night! More love and kisses XXoooo

Jan. 13, 1933
Sweetheart-

I shall start this letter this p.m. - perhaps I'll finish it now- perhaps not. But then, I'll add more tomorrow before getting it off to you.

Last night it was real mild and rainy - but during the night it blew up a mean and cold west wind and now it is exceptionally cold and snowing like the devil. One feels it so after the steady, mild weather we've had of late.

I should like to have seen you and your girlfriend lost in the subway. Err- that is of course if you don't look to worried or frightened. I know I'd have a hard time finding my way about so I shan't say too much about that!

It's along in the afternoon and I don't feel so well. The damnable cold has me again. I'll stick it out one way or another- Must..that's all!!

In order that you might receive this Saturday, I'd best close for now and get it off to you.

All my love for YOU!
Park

January 16, 1933
Darling Marie-

Only a few lines to let you know that over the weekend I was exceptionally good- did not drink a thing. Possibly it was because

I didn't feel so good anyway Saturday night after work. Wasn't last weekend perfect, though? Really.-I don't believe I've ever spent a more enjoyable one. Yes- and dammit- we're going to have another such weekend when we go to Rose (NY). Think not? Gee, honey- really - you're the only thing I have on my mind lately - just YOU dear. What's that? And why do I skip around so- dear- explain! Well, I can and will one day- I hope.

Sunday was beautiful- full of sunshine- in the p.m., I took long walk about 6:30, boarded the bus and went into town. Thought I'd go to a show but instead just walked around town and returned home at 9:30. The shows didn't look that great.

Charles Stanton came home Sat p.m. and he was just over here for a haircut and shave. He didn't look too good...lost 40 pounds- doesn't look like his former self. I hated to see him out of doors so soon but maybe he knows what he's doing.

Yesterday I walked over to the Shell and obtained a gallon of gas. My old can was quite empty so I had to pour some into the vacuum tank to get it started. Ran it a while til it charged the battery but didn't dare go into the street, The troopers would have come along surer than hell. Anyway... found the motor still runs (not runs still!) so I'm all set except for the license plates!

Well, in a bit over 3 weeks you should be returning, The time is surely flying by quickly- won't seem long at all now.

My business is pretty well shot since Jan 1. I guess all businesses are running accordingly- no money being spent anywhere. Would like to see things pick up a bit bt I guess we need to sit tight for that.

Gee- I have a bad cold in me 'ead for about 3 days and it's not a bit comfortable. Feels like me old noodle is being squeezed in a vice. I believe I'll take a snooze in my chair now so will close-

All my love-
Park

January 20, 1933
My darling Marie-

Before retiring and as I listen to Barlow and his symphony orchestra, I shall attempt to write a few lines to you that you might be assured that I'm thinking of you once more and that I'm anxious more than ever for your return to our fair community. Quite a sentence, eh? I should sleep quite well after that one! Eh... wot!

My business was a bit more brick today but I don't exactly kill myself from labor. It's awful how dull the old town has become since the 1st but at least I'm on the job and trying hard- that's all one can do, isn't it?

The "dog" was around after I finished work - suggested that we get a wee drop or two and I said," Nuttin' doin." BRAVO,huh? Well, instead I went over to the poolroom and played three or four sociable games with a chap. The "hound" waited and watched for a time but I guess he finally got tired and went home- and so-- after the game, I came home and quite alone. Glad?

Haven't seen any of your folks of late - suppose I have been busy when they've been to town on their usual shopping tours. Anyway- I'll keep an eye out for them- perhaps I'll see them tomorrow.

My old nose isn't like it was- rather drying up as it were- -and I'm feeling rarin' to go. Think not? Only 3 weeks left to go- and, well- use your own judgment. Let me warn you though, big girl- there'll be no more clinches and pinches in the dark- gee whiz! And, yes- I suppose I shall have to start another moustache sprouting soon. I'll sow the seed tomorrow- the moustache seed. Rare stuff. If that's the only seed I sow, you won't kick much, will you?? Just wait until you get here. I'll fix you this time- ah- shut up! No- honey- I'm a changed man- -no more violent love orgies for me- not much.

Well- sweet, I'm going to retire early so nighty-night for now.

All my love-

Park xxxoo Silly but this is supposed to be a letter anyhoo.

Jan. 27, 1933

Darling-

I only arrived home from work less than an hour ago which means I'm behaving at least one mere night. Ain't that something, though?

Received your nice letter this a.m. and it sounds so nice when you speak of your homecoming. Gee whiz- maybe 2 weeks from this very hour we'll be together. Boy- Oh Boy- I can hardly wait!!

Saw you mom and Dorothy pass by today. I was so busy that I had not time to talk to them. Gosh- maybe you had better purchase a couple of games for you and me- if I don't have my car going, we'll have to amuse ourselves somehow,- what'd ya think? Oh, well- possibly we can find games here- 'nuff said

Gee- have felt mean today. Get so moody at times that I must be unbearable to those about me but I can't help it. When I'm in such a bad mood, I feel out of place- should be alone in the woods somewhere, I suppose. The stress of being the only bread winner is getting to me. So many depend on me.

The "pup" was around tonight and did I use him mean? Gee- he gets my goat at times- I believe I'll end up busting him on the snozzola. Guess I've humored him too much-now he expects me to go out with him regularily. Well- me fool him- me fix- me go where I pleeze. So, tonight I came home and left him.

I've had a hellova a job trying to keep the home going- business is so damnably rotten- I could jump into A lake and love it, That is- if course- if you weren't returning home soon. When I think of that, it rather changes my spirit a bit- so, for heaven's sake- don't remain away too much longer.

Well, sweet, must hit the quilts so cherrio for tonight

Park xxxxxooooo, ah- hell- all the kisses I have for you!.

Feb. 2, 1933
Darling Marie-

You letter came this morning- so glad to hear from you again. Gee, sounds nice- that us when it' so near your time to come home. One week from to night instead of 7 days off. Oh, well- won't be long now. Guess I can wait another little week after waiting this long- guess I can be good too. Exceptionally so- what d'ya think?

I really don't know about Charles and Rose. Either yesterday or the day before, I saw Charles standing by the bridge waiting for a ride, I suppose. I haven't talked to any of your family at all lately so I couldn't tell you a thing. Gee- I suppose I shall have to live at your house for a while to sort of re-acquaint myself. No- I guess I shall have to stay at home- that is some of the time. But, I intend to leave your home at 10:00 at night... I say "intend"...what do you think? O well- dammit-, we must wait and see. Wish to hell time would improve so that we might have more enjoyable times together- but- hell- brother, can you spare a dime? Things are pretty tough and you're mighty fortunate that you are walking back to your old job at Crouse. Wish I were more gifted in "chiseling" but- well- I won't chisel from a nurse 'cause I really 'ates 'em- no I don't- yes I do- all but YOU. Ah, shut up park. You're different - just wait till you get here and you'll see..ho hum!

It has been miserable out today- raining- half snow and half rain. I've actually had a good week til now, but I'm afraid I'll lose out today. Anyway, I am plugging forth each day and that's about all I can do, n'est-c pas?

Listen, honey- I've a lovely kiss on my lips waiting for you. I'll start the moustache soon and maybe it'll be redder than ever. IF so- use your judgment

Hurry home to me- can hardly wait!

All my love-

Park xxxooooo.

[In February,1933, Marie has completed her course work at Brooklyn Medical College and has returned to Crouse-Irving Hospital, Syracuse, NY. She has been appointed Supervisor of the Pediatric Unit]

Feb. 15, 1933

Sweetheart-

Received your letter this a..m. - gee- seemed so good to hear from you again. So, you will be on days for 2 months? Well- we must figure out meetings accordingly then, mustn't we? Tonight there will be another orchestral concert at the University which I should like to hear but things are so quiet here that I doubt I can afford it. Anyway-honey- I shall try to come out one night this week- maybe we can take in the Regent (movie theater) or something. I had hoped that no one would be in the shop Monday when you were in - but- guess you brought business with you and I stayed busy 'til closing time.

Last night I went immediately home and at 9:45 I retired for the night. Really! I'm going to quit spending my time and money on booze. I can't afford it and it's so foolish. You said you liked me better when I'm sober, so I'm going to try awfully hard to comply with your desires.

I know it must seem quite lonesome there for you- especially at first. Wish I could come out every night but then, we'll just have to do the best we can by coming out once in awhile. It won't be too long now until spring and then I hope we can see each other more often. HMMM?

Glad you have been placed in such a good job- how does it feel to be "da bigger da boss"? More power to you honey- keep up the great work.

There isn't much more to speak of. I'll try to call one night real soon- If business is good one day, I'll be alright. I will be in at night. Will probably give you a ring first though. I'm being good, honey. From now on I am thinking only about YOU constantly. Write again.

All my love and kisses just for you-
Park xxxooooo

Feb. 20, 1939 Funnyville, NY Monday p.m. Sweetheart-
'Good afternoon...are you glistening? All is well.

After leaving your pleasant company last night, I walked immediately to Fayette Street and caught that old bus. I was lonesome though- don't you forget that! I really don't know what makes the time speed so when I'm with you but it surely does! It goes too fast, hmm?

I was abed by 12:30 and awoke this a.m. - feeling fresh as a newborn pumpkin- figure that one out!

Received a card from dad this a.m. stating that he left Florida on Friday last and that he expected to reach home Tues. or Wed. sometime! Gee- hope he's feeling well enough to relieve me a bit- BOY! I need some rest or- in other words- to be with you oftener- more Marie and less booze. A remarkable prescription...huh, Doc? I really have no desire for the booze- feel dandy today. Glad that our weekend was so great minus that!

Gee, dear- hope you aren't having tummy aches of too severe nature. Feel so sorry- wish I could be of some assistance - but how? O, well, we'll be better next week.

Can you imagine it...The clouds have disappeared from the skies- the sun is actually shining out once more. What could be sweeter? Nothing, save a bright summer's day with you. O it won't be long now, will it? Let's hope not.

My grand dad says he feels better today but he's not his real self. His appetite is poor, and he can't get around like he did a short while back. Poor old man- says he hopes not to die till the weather gets nicer.

Gee- old age is certainly tragic.

Gee- honey- I really don't know which night to visit you again. Perhaps it's best that I wait til after Wed. until I see when my dad returns. You know- I'd like to come out every night but gee whiz! Oh, well- no doubt I'll have my 'orseless carriage going after a while- then it'll be easier - you know how 'tis!

Cherrio for now- all my love, toujours!

Park xxoo and sooooooo many more

February 27, 1933

Morning Little Buttercup-

Gee- if you think it isn't frosty out here in the sticks this morning- you're a bit off. Have been thinking about the unfortunate "break" we had last evening- dammit- really- I had no intention of being selfish, but-I guess that's life. Can't be contented always can we be? I'll see that the Suburban (bus) puts on a special bus leaving here at 12 midnight after this - a special bus just for you. A lovely thought, don't you think?

Rolled that tin into the shop last night and it's a mammoth thing- still don't know what to do with it now. There's enough rubber in it to make 8 tires for my car-- don't know- perhaps I shall toss it into the creek yet.

When I returned home last night, I did nothing but retire immediately. And, did I sleep! Think I didn't? I know that it was hard to crawl out into the cruel, cruel world again this a.m. Gee, the night seemed to have passed nearly as quickly as the time did when I was last with you. Gee- I can't figure out just where the time goes, can you?

My dad just came on the job - he has been helping mom do the wash this morning. I might have had that job but I was afraid that it might give me too much experience which might prove to be too handy at a later date. Baby diapers, etc. O, gee- I'm trying not to be silly like that again. 'Scuze please. It was merely a little slip, honey. BUT- I must watch those slips, Here ever after, what do you think? Can't tell though- the women are commencing to wear the pants- we poor males must do something, you know. Maybe we'll wear the skirts soon. Consequently, then we'll have to do the intended work which nature bestowed upon the female. I say, wouldn't that be a pity?

Dammit, I really don't know whether I can get in to visit you before Thursday night or not. I'd like to awfully but will just wait and see what happens with business. Gee- I get a lonely old feeling, too, and it's far from pleasantness. Anyway- spring is only around the corner and that weather will help a lot when it arrives.

How's the old back this morning, sweetheart? Any new itchy spots develop? I'd really like to scratch it for you right now, but you know how 'tis!

Well, little pigeon, I must get busy for a change right now. So, cherrio- -for now. Be see'in you.

All the love I've got- for YOU.

Park P.S. Will remain awfully good until I see you again- and even better when I am in YOUR company!

March 1933

Darling-

I suppose I should be too ashamed to even attempt to these few lines to you- anyway I must offer my humble apology. If you accept it, I'm sure I don't blame you the least. When I awoke this a.m., it was like awakening from a miserable dream- worse that that even- a nightmare perhaps. My memory is vague as to what words we exchanged last night - I do remember that you panned me out and I do beg of you that you see me on Thursday night that you might-give me merry hell which I deserve so much. I assure you that I'll be sensible Thurs.

Park xxxooo

March,1933

Sweetheart-

Just came home for lunch so will write these few lines as a dessert. Will it taste like ice cream? I wonder. Anyway- I'll have to ask you Sat. night and Sun., won't I?

Anyway, all is set for the big Sunday dinner, so leave a bit of a hole for it. Maybe I think we cook 'um a nice chick- you like-a chick? Hmm, we cooking funny- takum off feathers- stick in pot- big appetite- hmmm-eat a too much- we get a -sick!

My dad is on the job today - doesn't feel too strong but is doing his best. Whatever 'tis that he has, has surely taken the pep out of him. It's really too bad that he couldn't have remained in Florida.

Gee - right after I opened the place this morning, I had three haircuts in a row- maybe business will pick up a bitta better, huh? Received a check from Boston this morning for $4, so now I must buy shows. Nice, huh?

Well, honey- I can make it in Sat. nite, ok? I want to- don't forget that. Hope to be seeing you Sun at 2:30 or thereabouts.

All my love always-

Park xxxooo

March 3, 1933

Sweetheart-

Perhaps 'tis a pity that I should be pestering you so soon with a note- but then- I'm sober anyway and that should mean something.

Last night I went immediately home and a friend of Grace's was there with plenty of "hooch" and when I said "no", my dad nearly collapsed! I left the party and went straight to bed right away. Now what do you have to say? Little pollywog! Go ahead and say it- for once I'm innocent- ye who accuseth me of guilt! Eh!! Humbug! ..not hamburg. I'll bet I was in bed before you last night- or at least I have a hunch I was. What' d'ya think? Oh, yeah!

Listen, all else aside- I'd rather be in a serious mood about staying out tomorrow night- sort of planning it anyway. I shall call your mom at 5 Saturday evening and if I can't quite interpret the meaning of your message, I shall call you between 6:45 and 7 to be certain. Right?

I'm just beginning to feel like myself today- that stuff didn't help a bit on Tuesday. You can jolly well gamble that I'm off the stuff through Lent. Not in a religious sense so much but mostly because I've come to the conclusion that I might just as well start reforming now as ever. In that way,maybe I'll be making a few individuals happy and - after all- that's the only way to show one's religion or creed- by making others happy. N'est-ce pas?

Anxiously awaiting news regarding Sat. night.

All my love always-

Park xxxxxooooo

March 6, 1933 Funnyville, NY

Sweetheart-

Well, here 'tis as I promised. All I have to do now is keep all my promises- sounds easy- perhaps it will be. Who knows? At least, I'm off to a wonderful start --nearly one week now and I still sit way up high upon the wagon. Gee- if I was to fall from this height, it would be terrible- possibly I'd break my neck and never be able to climb up again. Oh, well- let's not talk of such things while we have brighter things to speak of.

Your mom and dad just went in and out of the American store. I would have waved to hem a "hello" but didn't catch their eye- so, that's that!

I feel fine today and I guess it's safe to say that I'm raring to go once more. But- even if I'm raring, I can wait. Waiting is good for one at times, you know. Waiting is too easy though- especially when one is lying abed and waiting for 12:00 to come on Sunday! My! How the time did fly! Too damned fast, I think! Anyway, it was a perfect weekend with nothing to mar or interrupt it - uh, hum. That is- this far! Don't be alarmed though- I can think of some pretty names.

Once more we should speak of pleasant things .IT is pleasant to speak of spaghetti, may I ask? Well- I think 'tis and wish I had a huge portion of the stuff staring me in the face right now. Why, I wouldn't mind if few strands would stick to my ears or even my "mustn't touch it"! That would be too bad for sure! Red spaghetti and a red moustache- a lovely match. Oh, yes- and Marie's red lips - a dandy combination. Not the artificial red lips though- gee, that might prove fatal. However, I suppose I'd take a chance even though it meant death.

Business is frightfully dull today. In fact, there isn't any such animal. I'll probably remain thus throughout the bank holiday- til Friday anyhow!

Well- honey- can't think of anything further to interest (or was it?), so I'll sign off for now. Don't know about Tues. night but I'll do my best- if I'm there, I'll try to come early.

Did you hear the one about the barber who was afraid he'd get a "weak end" over the weekend? Well, never believe it! Thanks to Mother Nature!

Toodle-do- all my love-
Park xooo

Funnyville- March 17, 1933
Sweetheart-

Your letter awaited me when I reached home this afternoon and gee whiz! I had so planned on seeing you tonight. Ah, well- I guess tomorrow night will do as well. Hmmm? I've rather a cold today anyway and perhaps by tomorrow I shall be rid of it- hope so at least.

Yes- I reached home quite safely on Tuesday night- however, I hated to leave you at that cruel doorway. Took the bus home. In that way I felt more certain of arriving home ok. Can't tell where I might end up by travelling in pleasure car, especially when the driver is pleasure bent. I've been so good lately; I hate to slip now... think not?

Maybe tonight I come in- maybe no come. Went to bed early last night and I suppose I can do it again tonight.- because it wasn't such a bad dig after all- just like a kiss that shows. See ya tomorrow. Until then...

Toodles. Love and kisses and a bit of cherrio!
Park

April 10, 1933
Dearest-

What an elegant day this has turned out to be! A pity we can't take a walk. Guess one must stay in- doors and like it.

My dad feel much improved today - is up and around the house dying to walk out in the ozone but I told him he had better stay inside another day or two. If he is able to be on the job Wed. I shall try my damn- dest to see you. If this weather continues, I believe all will be ok- hope so. Well, I wonder how old _____ is? (The lecherous old guy!) Every time I think of it, I get a laugh. Really, it's the most absurd thing I've seen in years- actually silly Oh, well- it's all in a lifetime!.

Will try to plan Wed. night about 8. If I'm not there by 8:15, you'll know it's off.

All my love always-
PARK

48 Strathmore Rd, Brookline, Mass
My Darling Marie-

Well, here I am in the land of sunshine and beans- as yet I haven't seen either! But, no doubt I shall see both before I leave.Our trip was quite enjoyable - We left Fayetteville at 8:15 and reached here at 7:15 Tonight

Am so hungry for a letter so don't wait too long after knowing the address please!.

Love you-

Park xxxooo

48 Strathmore Rd, Brookline, Mass

Darling-

Have you any stationery like this? We also have a great assortment, but the news is news no matter what if the paper matters, I'll quit right now. Well, then, we shall proceed.

Aw- gee- honey- your letter came this a.m. and I was tickled! Was I tickled? I'll say I was - seemed darn good to hear from you. Boy- I have been real lonesome for you- miss you like the dickens!

Today, Mike [Gen's husband] and I saw the relics, antiques, etc. I enjoyed it alot- All so new and Different! We took the Plymouth off the dealer's hands. Gee- it'ss a peachie car. This p.m. the three of us went riding - we went over to the harbor- saw the fishes at the aquarium, etc. All was a real treat! Oh, yes- before we got the car this a.m.,Mike and I dropped into a couple of historical buildings. I enjoyed it all- and so inter- esting.

Mike has to drive to Springfield Wed. so perhaps I'll go with him and then on home. They want me to stay a couple more weeks but I don't know what to do. However, I'll make up my mind by Wed. If you were here, I'd love to stay forever and love it. And well- it's different knowing that it is an impossibility for you to be present. Maybe sometime we shall be able to go places together- what d-ya think?

Don't know what is planned for tomorrow but will let you know about it.

All the love I know for u. Cheerio- be seeing you soon.

Love, Park xxxooo

April 21, 1933 Mass

Sweetheart-

So far I've been putting my time to good advantage - but gee- honey girl- I miss you so much! Mike came home from Portland, Maryland last night and the 3 of us went downtown to the Loews theater and saw

Joan Crawford in "Today We Live"- a splendid picture. Can find my way around in the subways already - simpler than in NYC.

This afternoon we went down and Mike purchased a new Plymouth sedan which he will get tomorrow at noon. It's a pretty blue- nice to look at. Sunday, no doubt- we'll go places in it and in that way I can see points of interest in Boston and vicinity. I'd like to grab off a chunk of Bunker Hill for you but perhaps won't get a chance! I'm quite interested in seeing more historical places. I think they'd be nice to see with you- HMM?

Wish I could be with you Sunday- I know I shall miss you awfully. It's a terrible feeling - this heart sick feeling you get in the moments of loneliness, isn't it dear? You needn't worry about me and any old females here -haven't seen any that would appeal to me at all. You overshadow all the rest, honey!

I was just thinking of Almond Street and funny things, etc. Guess I shall never get over that- it was so odd and humorous. Doesn't it still make you laugh a bit?

Well, honey bunch- I must walk down and mail this and shop a bit for our supper. I'm anxious to hear from you- maybe I will in the a.m. Hope so cuz I'm so lonesome for you - little pigeon!

All my love always- forever and ever!

Park xxxxxxooooooo

Marie Darling-

My, oh my - what wonderful weather we are having in Boston. Very nice. Dammit- I'm like a fish out of water and I'm lost without you!

Sat. night Mike and Gen and I went over to the apartment of a young couple with whom Gen and I rode here. Had a good time. Highballs were served but I didn't over indulge for once. Just got a feeling of "glow" - that was it.

Yesterday WAS A LONG DRAWN- OUT DAY.Seemed that way anyway!

They took me to all these different interesting points in town and drove out to some beach. Guess that was near Walden. Thought of your friend there but perhaps it's just as well that you don't give me her address. HA! She wouldn't have mattered at all, YOU are the only one I'm thinking of - ONLY YOU

We were at the Bunker Hill monument and Mike and I climbed to the top of it- 294 stairs and what a climb! BOY! Too much for me. A wonderful view from the top, though. So, our efforts were quite rewarded.!

Guess Mike goes to Springfield either Wed. or Thrs. Think I'll go along with him and then home. Will call you as soon as I reach home anyway!

Love,
ME

May 5, 1933
Darling-

Merely a few lines while I am home for lunch to let you know that I still am a model litle boy! On the wagon- and what-not! I was offered a drink last night and turned it down flat- rather nauseated me to think of it. Say, by the way, I have been wondering of late whether or not you have been putting pills in my coffee- something has happened. I can actually say "NO" to booze and like it

Gee- this a.m. a card came from Binning and he has an $8 an hour job for me at Onondaga Hotel Friday night, May 12, so I can can start to practice right away. Maybe I can borrow a good horn somewhere- mine is about shot. Hope I can get several playing jobs before the summer ends.They'll come in handy, think not?

I'm anxious to find out about your mom, Expect me to be in tomorrow night as early as I can- will catch the bus at 8:22 at the latest but will try to make it before if possible.

Boy o boy was II tired last night and dd I retire myself early! Just ask me sometime if you think not. However-

Whoops- customers! YES!!!!!!!!!

Love,
ME

May 12, 1933
Darling Girl-

It is but 9 a.m. and here I am about to surprise you with a bit of nonsense and foolishness- of course- that is, if you don't mind. And if you do mind, you undoubtedly have read enough already and had better destroy this whole epistle

When I reached home, there was no party going on at all so I'll be damned if I didn't go to the ice box, scooped out a sauceful of lima beans and had a party of my own. And let me tell you- I put in a miserable night trying to sleep- I must have awakened no less than a dozen times. Consequently, no more beans for me! Henceforth- no more booze and beans and it must look to you as if I had no more brains! Sad thing- well- we shall see about the beans!

Be seeing you Saturday night, I hope. Perhaps we can find a few moments of seclusion somewhere. Until we meet again, doodle-do and all the love I have for you!

Je vous aime!

Park xxxxxoooooo,

March 15, 1933 Funnyville, NY

Darling-

No doubt you think I'm a bit cracked due to the fact that I write so often, but gee whiz! Don't think that, honey! Last night sped so quickly that I didn't get chance to say enough so I'll finish in this manner.

My dad feels much improved this a.m. - slept well last night. I believe he'll be going strong in about 2 or 3 days. If he only does what Doc Sam tells him, I believe he'll have no trouble at all

Harold Beach just came in and was kidding me about your being over there Thurs. eve. I said that yoU had told me about it, and that I was gunning for him yesterday, but gave up the chase as I left my gun home today.

A fellow tinkered with the radio here Sat. and now I am able to get WFBL faintly. It's better than nothing and the music helps me while away the lonely time.

It's nice out there a.m. - wish we could take another walk. It's mean to have to stick to the job on these pretty days, isn't it? But I expect in order to exist, we must do so.

Well, sweetheart- it's lunchtime so I'll post this on my way home. Hope to be seein' you Wed. or Thrs. Perhaps my dad will be able to relieve me Thurs night!

Until we meet again- Cheerio!

All my love-

Park xxxxoooooo

March 28, 1933

Sweetheart-

Last night returning home, I went at bed at once. And did I Sleep!!
BOY! I was dead tired- didn't know a blessed thing until 7:45 this a.m.
My dad didn't sleep well last night and so he will remain in the house
to recuperate. So, I'm on the job ane and at present- I'm real lonesome!
I hope the sun shines soon- the weather is too gloomy.

Well- I sincerely hope that your birthday was a happy one. Regret
awfully that I wasn't in a position to make it one of real happiness and
delight, But, perhaps I can do better next time. Yah? Anyway- I want
you to feel assured that my heart meant well!

You've grown so on me of late- what is it? LOVE? YES! No doubt
about it. Wish I were able to afford a castle, just for you. Yes, dear- a
castle high to sit upon the shores of the beautiful Limestone Creek - but,
as it is- well, the only castle I dare think of is this barber shop building
overlooking the Limestone Creek! Sorry!

Gee, whiz! Just had a haircut - wonderful- astounding- times are
picking up - wonder where the fella got a quarter? Anyway- I've got it
now- so that doesn't matter so much!

Gee - Liz (Marie's middle name, Elizabeth)- it's blowing and strike
me if it isn't trying to snow some more! And, say, Liz- think I don't feel
the cold. Aw gee- I'm sure I had nothing to do with it, little cucumber.
I'm awfully put out about calling you LIZ. "Scuse, please. But, gee -
your name could have been Elizabeth Marie as well as Marie Elizabeth!
I'm sure I had nothing to do with it!

Well, little pigeon- guess I'd better mail this right now and nap in
the barber chair..If things pick up, tomorrow night I shall be seeing you.
Dammiit! I get so lonesome for you!

Cheeerio! All my love,

Park

Friday a.m.

Mornin' Sugar-

8:30 in the morning and here I sits- pretty one- writing to you. What could be more absurd, my dear. I shall try not to be so silly- there now- is that better?

Gen left this a.m. about 7:30- she expected the Allens at 6 and the poor child had to wait 'til around 7:30. I awoke just in time to bid her farewell. Wonder why I slept so soundly. Or should I ask YOU that? 'Nuff of that.

By the way- sweetheart-- you remember last night that I said that I didn't want to see you so often? Of course- I didn't mean that! But since leaving your lovely company last night, things happened such that I won't be able to see you so much. Let me explain- please.

At 8 this a.m. Prowda came out and booked me to play with him Monday night in the N.R.A. parade. Probably $5/hr so there's Monday night I won't be seeing you. Tues. night I want to attend lodge (Masonic) -Perhaps you can see some of the parade and then see me afterwards. Hm, are you listening? So smarty nose- How 'tis? But the parade will begin at 7 so we can meet afterwards..

My car lights stayed lit last night and I hope my man appears in the scene this a.m. to find the real source of the ailment. I'd hate to spend 75 cents every night for bulbs, you know. You would too… Perhaps not..

Told mom about Turek this a.m. so perhaps after lunch I'll have to shoot her down to see him. The way business started out this a.m., I guess I won't be missing a thing. Perhaps I shall see you- perhaps not! Who knows?

LOVE-
ME

June 16, 1933, Hotel Hilton Butcher Shop
My Sweetheart-

How's this for a surprise? Thought I'd let you know that I reached home safely last night and went to bed immediately upon my arrival. Dammit. You know I hate awfully not to be in a position to see you tonight and tomorrow night. I'm even lonely already - it will seem an age til Sunday afternoon, I know. I can't figure out why FATE has arranged it that we should be so separated but it has nonetheless. Anyway- honey- it's not in line with my desires, remember that!

Mike is due to return tonight and they plan to leave tomorrow for Boston. From then on, I suppose my dad and I will become housekeepers, cooks, washerwomen and what not! Perhaps the experience will come in handy only for the purpose of showing my wife (should I get one) the hows and whys of housework. After I show her, I shall then stand over her with a ball bat to see that she doesn't rest too much. Niice fellow- don't you think? Perhaps my plans will have to be altered a bit when the time comes but I see no harm in making plans at present for the lovely future. What do you think?

Just finished calling my nurtz friend at Crouse Irving Hospital. A delightful little armful Gee- only a few years ago, I abhorred nurses- shunned them. But now- well- I still shun them all but one and she- o well- I'll tell her about it Sunday.

Gotta go...
LOVE YOU-
Park

June 23, 1933
Sweetheart-

Here 'tis 11:30 - went into town at 8 This a.m. and got my $2.80 at the Hilton. Purchased some barber supplies and went back to F'ville at 10. I'm not such a bad shopper, do you think? Had a notion to call you but thought your duties too heavy this a.m. and changed my mind.

This a.m dad mentioned nice things- spoke of going to Florida and suggested that if I became "hooked up" that I live in our present house and keep the barbershop going all winter. Oh, gee- yes. And he said that he likes Marie alot-- not kiddin'. Now I ask you- ain't that nice? So you see, Hotty makes all these stories up- nothing to it. Guess my dad thinks our affair is serious. Is it?!!!!!!!

Well, I'll tell you more about it Sat. night or Sunday, hmmm are you listening? Sat. night I went immediately home and my dada and I sat up until just after 11 and talked. He said nice things then, too. Tell you all about it.

Took back my "All Quiet on the Western Front" to the library this afternoon. Hated to part with it, but then

I got a chance to show part of it to you so I'm satisfied. Next will be "He Who Gets Slapped". Laugh that one off if you can!

Today is quite a bit quieter than it was yesterday- have in $1.00 so far and I just got back from lunch. However, I suppose there'll be the grand rush tonight as usual. Hope so- papa needs new glad rags,

You can wait for yours! HA! OH, gee, don't cry that way about it, mama? Here- here (he then tenders the struggling young nurse a $50 bill.) Oh yeah-a pipe dream? Huh? No. No- it's only a play, so don't get excited. O well!

Received a card from my mama this am .She sends her best wishes and also hopes your mama will be well soon. ..Does that sound like a child to say "mama"? Oh, well- we are all children frolicking in a meadow, hugging one another as we tumble about in a giddy glee- we roll- we kick- we sing so gaily. Then, life is all jolly rollicking joyousness. How's that? It'd better be good. It ought to be good as it's extracted from "He Who Gets Slapped"! Gee- I'm raving again! Too bad. Too bad.

Just to change the subject, I'll call tomorrow about 6:30, then perhaps we'll know our plans for Sunday. Hope we can do something grand and noble- don't you? Isn't it strange how the atmosphere of things change.

Gotta fly-

Love, Park xxxxooo

July 24, 1933

Top 'o The Mornin, Sweetheart!

These few lines will inform you that I went straight to be upon arriving home. Was I tired? I Was tired! Gee- I didn't know a thing until morning. My dad was sleeping out on the lawn in the deck chair when I reached home but I was so dead tired that I never saw him. Grace, mom and Bill were out to some beer garden on Grand Avenue somewhere. This a.m. they raved and raved over it. The place had German folks who danced and staged entertainment. Guess we must try out this place when we go out again. And listen, honey- I'm not even going to indulge in beer unless you're with me. Just can't trust myself at all. Gee- I even feel week and bum today- but the worst is over. Guess I shall be able to get on my feet again now without troubles and when I do, I'm never stopping again. You heard that once before but my intentions are the best- believe that. Believe that!

Hope you enjoyed your swim the other day. I hope that you aren't burnt this morning. Gee, we didn't stay long enough for you to become severely burnt. Roy can say that his burns are never sore but I'd hate to have them just the same. I was like that once and believe me- I never want to go thru that again. Gee, I have sense enough not to repeat certain experiences- dammit! If I could only use my bean to as good advantage regarding other things. O well, we shall see.

You will excuse lease if I appeared sarcastic yesterday- I'm sorry. I will try not to be so again. Really- I feel so rotten- everything is my own fault.

I'm going to blow my horn each day from now on- enough to keep in condition anyway. Can never tell when a job will happen! Well- little buttercup-chances are that I shan't be in tonight but will be seeing you tomorrow. I hope either in Fayetteville or at the annex.

Until then- cherrio- All my love-

Park xxooooo

August 20, 1933
My Dear Marie-

Merely a few lines to surprise you and also inform you that I was in bed by 10 last night. What think'st Thou? Possibly I'm beginning to learn something, who knows? Perhaps- it's about about time that I did! Think Not?

My sister and her beloved husband departed this morning and no doubt they are on their way by now I thought possibly they'd leave that car radio for my amusement but no such good fortune. Oh, well- I'll let you buy me one for Christmas maybe.

O yes- while at lunch yesterday, relished some applesauce made from the apples given me yesterday. Thought of you and your mother as the stuff ran down my throat. A lively thought, don't you think?

The old village looks deserted this afternoon- wish you were here to brighten up m moments my little barrel of sunshine! Little keg, I mean- not barrel! You're not so big- yet. By the way where are you going on the 4th? O, my, the 4th is already passe. Am I forgetful? It'll never happen like that again.

If I only had the afternoon off, I should like to take a cool, refreshing plunge into some nearby lake. That reminds me-did you notice if the diabetes victim, My VanZandt, is at your hospital no not? Poor fellow- I must try to visit him one time soon.

Well- little buttercup- here's business so I shall await a reply concerning Wed.

Lovingly,

Park

Funnyville, NY August 29, 1933
Sweetheart-

Merely a few foolish and unnecessary lines to let you know that is Wed - a nasty, rainy day- a day filled with loneliness and misery. A day when one craves companionship of quality. Then why aren't you here? Very well then- I shall wait for tomorrow - a real companion then, eh?

This afternoon my dad went home and slept- I drove Mom to Manlius, picked up grandpa- drove on to Suburban Park- drove past the pavilion and then immediately out again and hone. The grounds were terribly wet and the whole resort looked dead. It certainly was a miserable day for a picnic. No doubt Fred Searls took a licking. And so we brought the old man to Funnyville and I just now reopened the shop. I await patiently for the business. Looks like I'll wait for sometime, too. But we should worry? Tomorrow you'll be here and all will go well. Perhaps you'll accept these silly lines in a cheerful way- might as well. Laugh a little, pant a little-cry a little. That's LIFE!

Life-my dear - is is mystifying, isn't it? Death is one of a mystery. Love- well love is so like an inflating rubber balloon- it starts out so flat- grows- grows- blows. Gets bigger and fatter - yes-and often it bursts- but sometimes it expands to the ends of the Earth. 'Tis nice - though-- n'est-ce pas? Fascinating- ever new- ever thrilling. At least it SHOULD be that way. I, for one, should hate it to be otherwise- shouldn't you? Oh, well-I shan't talk further on such a big subject. We're too ignorant- all of us- to try to approach such a subject.

By the way, how would you like to be slapped down by a huge Ontario wave right now! Wouldn't that be sad honey? Why, honey, do you think I'd let such an angry wave hurt you? No sir! I'd smash it right back so hard- o gee. Such a nasty day today. Will close-

Love, Park

Marie and Park were married secretly in 1936. In order to retain her nursing job, she must have remained unmarried! (At this time, school marms were supposed to be unmarried, also!) However, Nancy Elizabeth was born November 16, 1939. Sally Jane came along December 20, 1941.

Parker Gladden died May, 1961. Marie Hamilton Gladden died in 1971 after a courageous battle with breast cancer. Marie worried

that the grave plots at Oakwood Cemetery, Syracuse, NY(where her mother and father are buried in the Hamilton Family plot) would not be side by side , but, rather head- to-head. Park would comfort her saying, "Don't worry -Honey- I can always reach over, and pat you on your head."

INTERVIEWS WITH SURVIVORS OF THE GREAT DEPRESSION

Originally I got the idea for writing my play, "Geepers, I Love You" from the many unique letters my dad wrote to my mother while they were courting in the early 1930's. While I was directing the show for The Sullivan County Dramatic Workshop (2007), I began speaking with local folks who had survived the Great Depression Era. I found these interviews to be informative, sad, humorous and insightful. History reveals an unfortunate time when U.S. citizens, in particular, had to deal with the reality of these Depression years.

Memories of the 1930's by Hern London. DOB 1/04/28.

Although I have fond memories of riding in the rumble-seat of my uncle's 1920s car, playing miniature golf diagonally across from our Bronx, NY apartment building, going without power during the 1938 hurricane, etc., most of my recollections are of the inexpensive entertainment available to us through radio and motion pictures.

The local movie theater only charged 10 cents for kids before 5 p.m. My mother did not attend movies on "free dish night," but we all liked to go there on "Screen Night." This was a version of "BINGO". The one "better class" movie theater in our neighborhood, The Park Plaza, had a Wurlitzer organ that would rise from the pit and an organist would play while we all sang along with the lyrics projected on the screen. We "followed the bouncing ball!"

On the other hand, radio was my favorite entertainment. Not only did I listen to the cereal - sponsored serials in the late afternoon, I enjoyed the comedies, the mysteries and quiz programs on air almost every evening.

Because we lived in New York City, I wrote away for free tickets to attend every possible radio show, "live" in the studios of "Radio City," in downtown Manhattan. Is it any wonder why I became a college audio-visual director? I'm also an old-time-radio/old movie "Trivia Buff" to this day.

Interview with Ray Tunquist at this home in Florida, NY, March 2, 2007. DOB 8/25/1917.

Note: In response to my article published in The Hudson Valley Senior Gazette, Ray sent me a letter saying that he would be interested in sharing his experiences. This man is such a FUN GUY! Thus, a marvelous adventure began as I interviewed Ray!

The Letter: 2/23/07
Subject: Depression kids

I was born 8/25/17… 3.4 billion heartbeats ago! My first job was after high school with the R.E.A. I earned a few credits from Kent State, then to Ashland College for two years. I got my private pilot's license through the War Training Service. Joined the Air Force as a cadet 65 years ago- right after Pearl Harbor. Transferred to the Navy, then to Miami U, then to western Michigan U. Received my Navy wings 6/23/43 at Naval Air Station, New Orleans. Served as Flight Instructor and V.R.F.1, a division of Naval Air Transport Service. As a Navy pilot with flight pay, Lieut. Sr. grade- made $3,290 per year. I was discharged, 11/4/46.

If you wish to interview me, please hurry as I no longer buy green bananas and I have to pay in advance for 3 minute eggs!

Ray

The Interview:
I was born in Ohio and I lived on a self-sustaining farm. There was a crossroads, a gas station, a general store, a post office and a blacksmith's shop. I know "The Village Blacksmith" by Longfellow and I used to be able to recite it all. But, don't ask me to recite it now!

When I started school, we had a horse-drawn carriage. We had straw at our feet in order to keep warm. It had curtains on it, too.

For a few years, our toilets were outside. Then, they were built indoors later and we had to post signs on all the privies, "DO NOT USE!" The school housed grades 1 to high school. It was like a huge family. There was a brand-new auditorium and a gymnasium.

There was a story about OUTHOUSES. Eventually these were used for storage once they built in-door plumbing lavs. As the story goes, one of the girls went inside to use the privy. And a painter was inside. He painted right across her rear end as she was seated on the privy hole! She never forgot that! This story remains even though I don't recall her name. Yes- we used Sears catalogs then... not the hard pages, though. Regarding using a corn cob- first, you'd use a red one. Then a white one to see if you needed another red one. And the glossy sheets were no good either!! You'd wrinkle up the sheets into a ball.

I had the same teacher for grades 1 and 2. Then, when I went to high school, she went back to college. At that time, a teacher could have 2 years of college. She was the same teacher I had for American literature and grammar...Maude Edwards. She was very good. I recall many poems. She was also the dramatics teacher. She put on a junior class play but I was NOT the lead singer. For our final exam, we would stand in front of her class and recite. She'd give the author and the title of the poem and then we would have to recite the full-length poem. Yes- we respected the teacher - and each other!

My first day of school- I was 6 years old. My mother asked me how I liked it. I said, "I liked and I met a boy I liked very much! He asked his name and I said "John F", and she said, "I went out with his father before I met your father!" THAT was VERY disturbing to me! I thought, "My name could have been Forestneigger!" It could have been me! Or, perhaps neither one of us would have been here! And then, how would the world get along without US?!

As an aside- our current family doctor has operated on me a couple of times. I met him not long ago and he asked, "How old are you now?" I replied that I had heard that he had a remarkable memory. I asked him if he knew "The Gettysburg Address". He said, "Sure!" Remember that he had just asked my age. He began, "Four score and ten years..." And I interrupted him. "Hold on," said I, "You already made a mistake. It's four score and seven. And that's MY age right now!"

My mother died in 1930. I have two brothers and a sister. I came home from school and she was very sick. She asked for her pills and I gave then to her with water. She dropped the glass and she laughed about it. As I was cleaning up, I then looked at her- she was dead. She had a stroke!

Yes- we had a telephone- a stand up ringer box-type thing with batteries in it.

My sister had quit her job to take care of my father and us kids. School had started and we had a brand-new principal. He was a handsome young man. My sister and he hit it off a bit. He then married my sister in 1930 or '31. There were about 40 students in my high school for all four grades. He was our principal and made $2,400 a year! He wanted to save up enough money to become a lawyer- which he did do. They didn't want to get married right away until he got out of law school. As principal, he was VERY, VERY strict. Everyone liked him. His name was Henry _____. But for some kids who got out of line, he'd take the kid the office where he would use "the board of education," (aka paddle). And they never again wanted to visit the board again! I never did get the board. I tell you, he had discipline.

In grade school, all the teachers were females. For grades 5 and 6, I had a male teacher. In early grade school, I wore knickers and socks that came up to here (Ray gestures to his knees). I remember those socks because we had geese and those geese would love to bite my legs...they loved my socks!

As small a school as it was, we had a fine baseball team. We were champions one year. I was on the junior high team and was sitting there watching the senior high championship game. The coach, who was disciplined and had scruples, saw the center fielder smoking a cigarette. He whisked him out of that game and called to me, "Ray, go in there and play center field." I replied, "Coach, I got a sore leg." To which he replied, "Get in there!" When I got up to bat, the ball went by me so fast that I never saw it! (In junior high, I never panned out as an athlete.) So, the 2nd and 3rd pitches came by and I swung and hit. And the damned right fielder threw me out at first! My foot was really hurting and I didn't get to first base on time! The coach never said anything- but I DID hit the ball. We won the championship game! In the baseball game, I just wore street clothes. It was the Depression; nobody had uniforms! They had uniforms for basketball but not baseball. I had my own glove and always played 2nd base. It was at that time that Cleveland had a 2nd baseman named Bill Cissell. EVERYONE called me Bill!

At our farmhouse, we had a rotary pump near the house. At the barn, we had a 13 foot well, a dug well. It had a hand pump on it to pump water for the farm animals. Then we put in a

Fairbanks-Morris gasoline engine. That was a great thing. We had a huge water tank for the animals. Dad had a filter that came down off the house when it rained. The filter system would clean out the dust that came off the house when it rained and then he'd put the cleaner water into this big cylindrical holding tank. Water came down through sand and charcoal. Then the water went into the cistern. Oh, we had beautiful, clear drinking water. We had a pipe going to the basement which was lower, so we had running water due to gravity. We had a big copper reservoir and we always had hot water in there. There was also the "room stove," a fairly large circular stove in the living room. We took baths about every Saturday night. That was in the wintertime. In the summer, we went swimming in the river. The railroad always follows the river.

One of the very first things I remember was when President Harding died. The railroad cars went right past our house. It had flags all over it. We went up to the railroad bridge to pay our respects.

Down below we had a shed where we made maple syrup. Dad would pour in the sap. It takes about 43-44 gallons to make a gallon of maple syrup. He'd pour it into the big vat and when he went downhill, he'd just pour off into this 500-gallon tank. I'd run downhill to where we made the syrup. Just turn the lever and gravity would take it on down; we didn't have to do much work there. We had a big fireplace there. It must have been 3 to 3 1/2 feet wide and 15 feet long. A shallow tank was on top of that. That's where we boiled the sap. We pre-heated the sap. My dad always had plenty of wood taken from dead trees in the forest- big sticks. We always had a huge pile of dry wood stacked up.

We had 4 horses for teams, a dozen cows, some young heifers and lots of chickens. When it was time to eat one of our chickens for Sunday dinner, I didn't like that at all. I would know the names of the chicks. We slaughtered our own pigs for pork. When we served these animals for supper, I "knew" them! I'd sit there and cry.

We had our own milk. My dad had Holstein cows. At this time, they'd sell for $125...now one would sell for $1,000. A milk cow was $75. We grew oats, wheat, corn and hay. We had a big garden. I recall it was in the spring of the year, very warm. The windows were open on our way from school and my dad was just spreading manure in the garden. I was so embarrassed that the other kids would think that I was eating food from the smelly garden. But, they were all farm kids anyway. We had a tomato vine that grew out of the outhouse one year. It had the most beautiful tomatoes but no one touched them! I was glad that I didn't like tomatoes anyway!

Hoboes and tramps would come along the railroad track. They'd ask for handouts. We did have one problem. A railroad Section man had sent up a boy to get water. It was housed in a combination engine and milk house. Dad would cool the milk in the milk house before we'd send it to market. Dad walked by the shed and the door was closed. Our collie dog- an excellent farm dog- was standing barking at the closed door. Dad tried to open the door and couldn't. He pushed on it and saw a man just standing there. He said, "Keep that dog away and I won't come back again!" The man stooped to pick up the pail of water and his coat got stuck. Dad looked under his coat and there was one of dad's wrenches. Dad said, "That's why the dog won't let you out. You're welcome to the water but I don't want to share MY tools!" The man got the hell out of there. Later, the Section man saw my dad and asked, "Charley, why can't we get water at your place anymore?" Dad told him why.

There was one time when a pig was slaughtered. All the pigs were out because the gate was left open. The collie rounded up all the pigs and put them back in by herself. My uncle was there and said, "No way!! Charley, I'll give you $50 for that dog." My dad said, "NO!"

One time we were at the Medina County Fair and we came home very late. There was a long lane at the side of the barn to the woods. On the sides of the lane, were cultivating fields. There was corn in the field. The dog wasn't anywhere. We went into the barn and the cows and horses were gone! Something was very wrong! Dad went into the woods and saw the trouble. The cows had broken down the fence and were in the corn field. The dog who was home alone knew that those cows did not belong in the field. She took the cows out of the field and herded them into the woods. They wouldn't go past her. Undoubtedly, she saved many cows. They would have eaten the green corn and died.

She was a great collie dog- bob-tailed. She would come into the house as she liked the warmth. We wondered what we should name her. I mentioned "Sally" and other female names. (Roy NOW has a dog named "Sally"). Someone said, "Betty." She jumped right up and liked that name. So, that was her name from then on. She went missing for several days and we believe she was stolen. But she came home with a rope around her neck. She had chewed through the rope and made it home.

We always had dogs. One time it was rainy and muddy, so dad laid down planks. It got to be warm weather and those planks were warping. I was running with at least 5 dozen eggs and the dog was running ahead of me. As I got to the boards- the dog was on the other end. I tripped and fell and then they became scrambled eggs!

When I was in school, I could go to the movies for 35 cents...a double feature. Just the other day, my wife and I were talking about that. Her mother would go to the movies and get a dish. We didn't get to the movies much. Around 1928, the talkies came out. Before that, we had silent pictures. I recall the first talkie. I saw, "Wings." I was sitting on the edge of my seat and seeing this pilot with his scarf blowing around. I'd never seen anything like that before.

We had a battery-powered radio, an Admiral. It had 3 dials to turn just to get it tuned right. My father would sit there LOOKING at the radio and we'd kid him about that. He'd say, "When someone is talking to me, I want to look at him!"

In school, I was captain of my pistol team. We learned defensive maneuvers. Later on, when I was married, we were doing some showing off. And my wife (this is the only one I've ever had!) was listening to "The Boston Strangler"- a series on the radio. She asked what she would do if a stranger broke into our home and strangled her! I replied, "Lock the door! Do you want me to show you what to do?" Then, I put my hands on her throat like this, and you put your hands on my throat. I took her hands and she had to come up with spread elbows. Now, when you're up there, you can bang him in the nose. She did that action and hit my nose really hard! I was lucky I didn't tell her about the knee action!

They called my dad "Tunney." At that time Jack Dempsey was fighting Gene Tunney. We went to our neighbors who had an Atwater Kent radio to listen to the fight. At that time, we couldn't afford a radio. There was a series of many tubes in that radio. You'd have to take the battery down town once a week to get it re-charged...cost you 50 cents.

There was a general store. They had a glass case, a rounded display case. In it were many pretty candies that we coveted. The huge candies were a nickel. We didn't have money for candy. We did make candy out of maple syrup. My sister and I would make fudge once in a while. Popcorn- we grew our own for use especially in the winter time. We'd keep it in the attic where it would be dry. We'd go down in the cellar for apples. There were "cracklings." We sold large 5 gallon cans of lard. We sold eggs to the general store. They were maybe 60 cents a dozen. We had egg crates- single - 15 dozen; a double dozen crate had about 30 dozen. Someone would come around and sell snake oil medicine. My dad's favorite was Sloan's Liniment. Depression Era slang: Gasoline was selling for "5 gals for dollar"; We made fun of that.

My family were Lutherans. When you'd go to church, the wife and small children (boys in knickers) went to the left side. The men would go to the right. A boy couldn't wait to wear long pants so he then would be able to sit with the men. Then, you wouldn't think anything of mother nursing her baby right in church. I saw more breasts! Nothing was thought of it because we were raised on a farm. It was natural to see cows and horses suckle their young.

Our fruit cellar - The house was up on hill and its cellar was below and cool. All underground. It was filled with apples, meats, potatoes, carrots and cabbage. The pickle barrel was always full. My mom canned every-thing. We had homemade butter. I churned it. The woodshed was built right into the house. It was huge, I'd toss some wood into the large box, and then there were 2 doors that opened up on the other side. You'd easily get the wood into the kitchen and then put it in the stove. The stove was a huge black, cast iron stove. You'd have to remove the burners to put in wood. You'd take the flat iron and wrap it and take to bed with you.

Medina, Ohio was the county seat. It was noted for its honeybees. A friend of ours went to China and they asked him where he was from. He said, "Cleveland." (the population was around a million at that time). He was asked, "Is that anywhere near Medina?" Medina was just a little burg...they knew about Medina because of the honey bees!

Mr. Root asked me to go into business with him at one time. He raised bees - queen bees. I did have about 15 of my own bee hives. Mr. Root brought out some of his bees to our farm. Along the railroad tracks were huge white clover plants and plentiful. It was through him that I became interested in bees and got some of my own. He gave me the "X,Y,Z" of Bee Culture -- big book! In college, I took public speaking. At the end of the year, the teacher took a vote to see who in the class had given the best and innovative speech. I had given the best- on honey bees! He asked the class -why? They replied, "He knew his subject so well and made it interesting."

My father had been a firefighter before he met my mother. He said that when the bell rang, the harness was ready. It was dropped on the horse, buckled underneath. He was ready to go.

Roosevelt had many privies built...especially in the South where hookworms abounded! I recall when beer became legal - I believe '32. People made their own 'hooch.'

"Ah hate war. Elleanoor hates war," was Ray's drawing out in a fine imitation of FDR regarding Fireside Chats. I liked Roosevelt! My first job was with the REA (Rural Electric Administration). I heard a job was coming up and went to my (then) future brother-in-law about going to college. I bought his old blue Chevy coupe. It had 2 wheeled brakes. I had to drive to Wellington, Ohio to apply for this job---about 18 miles. I had no driver's license...you didn't need one then. A few years before I was 13, my mother died. I had driven her to the doctor's and so forth. I had a booster cushion so I could see over the dash. My dad had a Model T with a gear shift. I pulled into a space and the brakes didn't work and I rammed into a plane. I parked and went to tell them that I had hit this thing. I told the owners that I would pay for it. I gave my name and address. At that time, damage could be fixed for $25 or so. I said that I had come to see Mr. Daniel about a job. The man said he WAS Mr. Daniel! When he hired me that spring, I told him I wanted to work for 3 months then I wanted to go to college. There were 4 men on the crew. I was a "SQUEAK"- they called the new guy, a Squeak! I drove the car. They'd get out VERY early in the morning and do surveying for the REA as to where they'd put the electric poles. When I was leaving, the boss asked me if I wanted to stay. He would make me head of the crew. But, I went on to college. And I could have been in the electric business! My brother-in-law went to Ashland College. That's where I went. My first year out of high school, I attended a local college in Ohio where I got some credits from Kent State University.

I had always wanted to fly. One day I saw on the bulletin board a notice that read: "Ashland College will teach 10 students to get the private pilot licenses." I applied for it thinking that I didn't have a Chinaman's chance in hell. But, I got it! I got my license in 1941! I had read so much about the wars. I knew war was coming, so I enlisted in the medical corps. I wasn't about to kill anyone! But then Pearl Harbor happened! Right away, I enlisted- it took a while for the paper work and references, school grades, etc..... for Aviation Cadet Program. I reported in February. There were 3 fields available- Kelly, Randolph and one in California. They were filled, so I went home sick. Then I got well again. I met the mailman each day. One day all my records came back to me. A letter read: "You are disqualified due to x-ray findings in your chest." At first, I wasn't going to apply but then I realized I was about to die! I went to the college doctor who said," Nothing is wrong with you. Some shade-tail in the Army doesn't know TB when he sees it." The doc was a Navy man. In 10 days, I was in the Navy!

So, I went through as a P5 Cadet. I went to Miami University and did some flying there...and again in Oxford, Ohio. The hangar burned down while we were there! I went to Cincinnati. We flew down over Kentucky. Guess they thought that we were Revenuers. I came back one time with a bullet hole through my wing, just missing the gas tank! They were burning chestnuts down there which didn't make any smoke Then I went to New Orleans Flight Instruction School. It was there I got my Navy wings, the 23rd of June, 1943. They then sent me to Memphis, TN where I taught flying to a year. I flew the old bi-wings. Then they sent me to New York state, The Division of Air Transport (VRFI). We flew new airplanes from out of the factory. Some of us were getting these orders to fly these big transport planes to the Pacific. My turn was coming up soon. Then Truman dropped the bomb; that was the end of that! A buddy of mine's last name started with "T" so we two were always together.

One day we went to mess hall. We sniffed and smelled mutton. We didn't want that! So, he said," Wanna go out for dinner?" We did. Then he asked me if I wanted to go bowling. So, bowling we went! And THAT is where I met my wife! When I saw her, I said, "That's THE one!" I don't think she thought the same...but...(laughter).

While flying, you need to take the stick like this and think waltz tempo. While teaching flying to a student, I had a talking tube that went from my mouth to his ears. He couldn't answer back. I was singing "Swanee River" into the tube. The boy went off to Pensacola, FL. When I met him much later, he saluted me. Then he thanked me for his lessons. He said, "One thing, sir, I'd like you to know. I have sung at the Met in New York City." And I had been singing to him! We laughed.

One time I was flying and took my girlfriend on the trip. She was a WAVE. Then, Tyrone Power came along in a twin-engine airplane and took my girl! He had his instrument rating. I lost MY girl to Tyrone! At this time, it was the largest single-engine plane in the world. Another time I took a WAVE flying in a bomber. We had a pilot, a gunner. So, this WAVE sat in the back with the gunner. When we had landed, she said, "I've been trying to talk to you ever since we took off." I replied that I never heard her. So, I asked her to show me what she did. We went into the plane and she showed me the tube in the back. She had pulled out the tube from underneath and had been talking in it. I said, "That's the relief tube!" It was her first-time riding. I told her that it was the first time the plane was flown and the tube had never been used!

Note: Our one-hour tape had run out. But, then, Ray told me more about his recreations and his toys during the Depression years on the farm;

We made our own entertainment. We made sling shots. We'd roll a tire around. We played marbles. Tying a tire on a rope and hanging it from a tree was our swing. We'd toss the balls from the paw-paw trees. Swimming was free in the river. I had a bike that I bought for $5. I was fascinated by magnets! We'd toss hedge-balls in open doors of the railroad train cars that passed by. We would all gather nuts for the winter.

Chores were never ending. For example, I'd mow the lawn at home and in the cemetery, beat the rugs on Saturdays, feed all the animals, and gather eggs. We made soap primarily from the animal fat. Farmers exchanged help and willingly loaned out their machinery.

This marvelous "young" man told excellent stories with exciting animation! We laughed...a lot! Ray is a born story teller. He then showed me his lovely wood furniture mostly made by him. These pieces of furniture showed much TLC! As we said goodbye, Ray was on his way to the nearby saw mill to work on his wooden creations.

Interview with Alice Verlini Picarello, January 4, 2007. Monticello, NY Senior Center. DOB 2/25/1925.

Alice lived with her family in Bronx, NY when she was young. Her widowed grandmother had a farm on Sackett Lake, Monticello, NY where the family would spend most of their summers. Other family members would motor to Monticello...especially weekends.

Uncle Jack, in particular, would drive up old Rt. 17 which was a two-lane highway then. They were always stopping as their mom was always feeling car sick. When Uncle Dan (who lived on Staten Island) would also drive up Rt. 17, he would point out the "throw up" spots from previous journeys. Passengers were amused by this news! Sometimes both uncles and Alice's father would drive up - rather like a car-safari. They would arrive in time for lunch and then about 5 o'clock they would all gather for dinner. 7 P.M. was bedtime for Alice. Kids were allowed to have coffee for breakfast which was very diluted with hot milk and a beaten egg. Winter days, we would skate on the lake. Sunday dinner was at noon and then all would pack up and drive back to the city. It was a lot of effort for such a short visit. At that time, the trip from New York City to Monticello took nearly four hours.

For a short time, Alice lived in New Jersey. and recalls going to the movies with her cousins. Movies then cost 10 cents. They would walk from Teaneck to Englewood- a distance of about 3 miles. But what movie treats there were! There as the news reel, short subjects, cartoons and a feature film - sometimes two feature films.

Alice's dad worked as bus dispatcher along with his brother-in-law who owned the bus line. This was the first bus line in Bergen County which later evolved into the New Jersey Public Service Bus Company. When Alice's dad became very ill, she moved permanently to Monticello, NY. Her dad, who served in WW I, was sent to a German concentration camp in Austria. That was where he contracted TB. Alice was 10 or 11 at that time. He loved to sing and he sang for his bride at their wedding. Alice was the only child in the family. She was treated like a princess! Although her mom was a seamstress and her aunt a tailor, she wore store bought clothes. She feels she was VERY privileged and treated like this princess. She never wore "hand-me-downs."

Often she and her mom would ride the ferry to New York City to visit the family. The ferry crossed the Hudson from the foot of the Englewood Cliffs to the dock at Dikeman Street. The ferry ride cost 5 cents. Once she and her mom walked over the Washington bridge from the Bronx to Ft. Lee...safely. The trolley, which cost 5 cents, would get them all over NYC.

In Sackett Lake, Alice attended a one room schoolhouse for grades 1- 8. Years after, the building was purchased by a hunting club and was used as such until a few years ago when it burned down. Alice recalls two of her teachers. Miss Florence Woods (who later became Mrs. Arthur Carroll) and Miss Dorothy Skinner who became Mrs. Andy Goodwin.

These were times when tramps, hoboes and other transients. Most were willing to work for food. After graduating from Monticello High School, Alice attended the Middletown State Hospital for Nursing. After graduating as a RN, she worked at the Monticello Hospital starting in 1946. Sometimes she worked at the Hamilton Avenue Hospital. The Monticello and Liberty hospitals merged and was called The Catskill Regional Center. She retired in 1990.

A lasting impression of the Depression years took place in her grandmother's house. Her grandmother was sitting at the dining room table reading The NY Daily News. On the front page was a picture of a woman looking at a casserole dish. The caption read: "Now they have food and can't eat it." It was about a starving family in New York City whose 9-year-old son had hung himself. He left a note explaining that there were too many mouths to feed in his poor family. By killing himself, there would be more food for his younger siblings. That was over 70 years ago and she still weeps when she recalls that. Her family was not devastated by the Depression as were so many then. Her uncle was a bank president and had many investments.

Hair for women accentuated the finger waves. Her own hair was cut in a Buster Brown style! A slang expression she recalls was "the IT girl!"

Alice recalls riding in a car in a parade for Wendell Willkie in the early 30's. Her family was Republican, and still is. In 1932, FDR took the reins of the US!

Favorite radio shows were "Amos and Andy," "The Shadow," and "The Lone Ranger."

This charming lady graciously finished her interview, smiled and went in to join the Monticello Seniors in their Thursday meeting.

Interview with Leah Mitchell at the Rock Hill, NY Methodist Church (on her birthday) DOB 1/28/21.

Leah lived in Kauneonga Lake, NY with her mom, dad and sister. "Back then, we had outdoor toilets. I had a girlfriend who everyone thought was rich. Her father built their outhouse with 3 different sized holes...one big...one medium and one small.

Saturday night was always bath time. My mother had a galvanized wash tub. In the winter time, my mother would open the oven door of the large wood-burning stove to let it heat up a bit while we took our baths. We always looked forward to Saturday nights to take a bath. My sister and I got our baths first, then mom and Dad. We had a stove that had a water tank on it. They would take their baths later once the hot water heated up.

We went to school at the Kauneonga Lake School which had three classrooms. They had school up to the 8th grade. We had to come into Monticello to go to high school. We were NOT picked up at our house; we had to walk down the hill to the post office to catch the bus. But for elementary school, I had to walk about a mile to get to school in the winter time. There were no "snow days." No matter how high the snow was, we trudged through it all to get to school. I could never wait 'til Easter because during the winter months we had to wear long johns with bumps in them. Then, at Easter we could take off those long johns.

I had a girlfriend whose folks had a summer home near us. They used to give me Harriet's clothes and they were really nice clothes. I believe I had two pairs of shoes.

My dad was a carpenter and worked for my uncle. In the wintertime, there was no outside work. It was bad as we ran up a huge bill at the general store on credit Then we would need to pay it off. My dad had a couple of pigs. He would go to the hotels and get whatever food was left over and give to the pigs to eat. That was good then he'd smoke the ham and he bacon. We always canned a lot of stuff. We picked blueberries and huckleberries. We brought home peaches. Everything was "put up for the winter" (canned). We'd make chili sauce from the tomatoes. I would help my mother with the canning. My sister wasn't much for doing domestic chores as she was a tomboy. She would rather go swing on the birch trees. My mother did all the chores and I helped... I hated dusting. My mother was a fanatic about keeping clean especially about dusting. She would admonish me if I missed a spot. She would look under chairs and tables and when I missed, she said to do it again!

The "bestest" thing was ...we had a drug store out there that was closed in the wintertime. We could not wait for the spring for them to open! We'd get an ice cream cone for a nickel. When Decoration Day came, we always got our ice cream. We enjoyed penny candies. I recall the first bread that we bought- Bond bread. It was sliced, too.

Since I lived on a lake, there was always something to do...ice skating in the winter or sledding...or swimming in the summer. In the winter time, we would build a fire outside at night. There were great hills for sledding. There weren't that many cars then so we didn't look out for traffic! I recall seeing "Gone with the Wind"- that was a long movie. We'd go into Monticello to the cinema. Radio was important- I still listen to music of this time! We would hear Lawrence Welk before we could ever see him.

I remember my first perm. The machine was huge with cords with those things that were twisted around the hair... Big round things with curlers at the end. I looked like Orphan Annie.

I had the same teacher for 1st and 2nd grades. I was a good student. It was different in those days. Our bus driver was Asa Barber- she was tough. When the kids acted up and were bad, she would stop the bus no matter where it was and the bad kids got out right there. She'd say, "Get home the best you can!"

My grandmother lived next door. She was paralyzed with a stroke and we always helped her. She was a real Christian lady!

There was a hotel up the road from us. In the summertime, we'd babysit the kids. I stayed at the Rita Hotel one summer as a babysitter. We helped with all duties- making beds, and helping in the kitchen. I did not wait on tables. There were two sisters there who waited on the tables. I would laugh because of Bill Driscoll and Tim. Every Saturday night, they'd go dancing at Skinner's Ridge. First, they'd go to the barn and take care of the cows. Then, they'd come to the dance and I would see the manure on their boots

My dad always had a hound dog for hunting... a rabbit dog. In those days, there was no such thing as dog or cat food; they ate what scraps were left over from our meals. I never liked chipped beef. My dad never liked spaghetti! We were meat and potatoes people!

I recall Eleanor Roosevelt and the way she spoke.

I had an aunt who lost quite a bit of money in the stock market crash. Those of us who lived in the country were not as affected as the city people. Tramps and hoboes would come to the hotels to beg or work. Many were from Pennsylvania. The hotels were the Kenmore, West Shore, and the Woodlawn before there was the Concord and Grossinger's. My mother worked at the Kenmore.

To survive, you needed to have faith and a hard work ethic. I would get $5 a week at the hotel. I recall this old Jewish lady who gave me a chicken and a dime to take the chick to the Rabbi. I walked through the town with this live chicken in a sack. I was crying and a man asked, "What's wrong?" I said that I was to take the chicken to the Rabbi. He said, "Give me the dang thing!" He took the chicken to the Rabbi who slit its throat. I cried.

I crocheted...made afghans and I made mittens for little kids.

Leah married in 1940 and had two boys. Her husband, in the Army, wound up in Los Alamos in convoys and taking bombs to the airport. They were never sure if the bombs were real or duds. It was an enjoyable interview with Lively Leah!

Interview with Margaret Dolan at her home, Grahamsville, NY DOB 12/20.1921, Eureka, NY

I was born in our farmhouse. My mother was a nurse.

In the early 30's, I was in Grahamsville Elementary School. It was a two-room schoolhouse where the Tri-Valley School is now. There were 4 grades in one room and 4 in the other, Because the school only went to 8th grade, we had to go to Ellenville High School.

While in the elementary school, you couldn't help but overhear what the other grades were learning. I learned easily and was pushed along and entered high school at age 12. My parents believed that I was too young to do this. I did go in January, 1935 after passing the Regents. I took courses such as typing, drama and public speaking.

Evelyn Hunsberger was the best teacher I ever had. She was recognized through the whole of NY. Her mother, Mabel Hill, lived to be 102 and was a Sunday school teacher. We had a Sunshine Club and would take boxes of goodies to shut-ins. Each little package was labeled for days of the week. In those days, you could buy a washcloth for 10 cents. There were all kinds of things that an ill person could use while shut in. It was fun! Once I did get one while I was sick. I couldn't wait to open it. Mabel Hill was our guide with that and took care of us throughout our youth. Evelyn, her daughter, graduated from New Paltz. In those days, you went one year and then you could teach for 3 years and get credit for your second year and then go back for your 3rd year. She came right out of New Paltz at 16 or 17 and taught us for grade school for 3 years. She then returned to New Paltz. They recognized that she was an outstanding teacher, no discipline problems whatsoever. They sent her all over New York state to demonstrate her methods instead of her having to take courses in her 3rd year. She passed away 2 years ago. I would visit her when I could. We would have 20 to 30 students in our classroom. But then, they were divided into grades. Some grades would have hardly any students. You'd hear everything that was going on in the upper grades. When I got in "The Big Room" where the older children were, I was in grade 4.

I now live on Smith Lane-- my maiden name is Smith. This area was all my grandfather's farmland. Back then, it was called "Eureka," which is no more; it was a small village taken over by NYC to build the Rondout Dam. A conveyance I took as from there to school when I was young because it was 2 ½ miles away.

We had gardens and a huge farm which my father couldn't run because he had asthma. So, a farmer and his family milked the cows. In the 30's, the city had not taken the farm yet. When this did happen, we were really depressed in the valley because there was no one left to come to our store or sawmill.

We owned a general store in Eureka and it was also the post office. We sold tools, groceries, clothes, kerosene from a barrel, and molasses from a barrel. Tea was in a big square box. You'd measured out what you needed and then weigh it. Sugar was measured out and weighed. Lots of penny candy - and I ate all the profits from this! I went to work as soon as I could but did not get paid. I was sworn in by my father- a notary- otherwise I couldn't have worked in the post office. I ate candy for my wages! In the store, we had dry ice for the Eskimo Pies, but no ice cream. What didn't sell that Saturday night my dad would bring home and we were delighted to eat it. It wouldn't have lasted the weekend.

People would help themselves to pickles from a barrel. Loads of people would gather around the old stove. I just loved being down there with all those people. They told such tales! Mother told father the year I was engaged, "You need to find someone else for the store. Margaret needs to learn how to boil water!" I was always at that store!

So many people could not pay their bills. Dad wouldn't talk to us about this but in the later years I would hear from customers who would say," Your father trusted us for 5 or 6 years." It may have taken several years for them to pay him back, but most did. Some would bring in butter for us to sell.... or eggs. We, at home, did not realize. We had milk from the farm, made our own buttermilk, we fed and butchered cows, pigs, etc. When we wanted dinner, my dad would just take a chicken and chop off its head. I watched as the chicken ran around the yard.

My dad's mother lived there and had a great farmhouse with at least 15 rooms because they had 11 children. My great-grandfather and his family loved in one side of the house and my father's family had the other side. They kept adding more rooms and made the kitchen larger. Imagine, 11 children (one died in infancy.)

We all had meat to eat, milk, berries of all kinds which we could sell at the store. We got things wholesale at the store. I didn't really realize that people in the 1930's were so hard up until years later.

We'd go into S. Fallsburg to the Rivoli theater a few times or to Monticello to the movies. Mainly we'd go to church in Grahamsville. I went to clubs there so I really didn't need to go into town.

My dad was a Director of the Ellenvillle Saving Bank so he went to meetings there once a month. We'd visit the doctor in Monticello because there was none in Grahamsville.

My aunt was the first female lawyer in Monticello, Sullivan County- Nellie Childs Smith. She had an office in Monticello and had her home there. She never married and would come to the valley weekends.

When grandmother moved out, they built a home on Woodbourne Rd. on 42. It had 4 bedrooms. The sisters who didn't marry came home weekends. Aunt Harriet was a teacher. Aunt Mary was a teacher but didn't really like it, so she came home to work at the post office and store and took care of mother and dad when they got elderly. But the big home in the valley was so beloved by us all. It had a front porch almost all around it, 3 sets of stairs- one in each wing and then the front stairs. They had indoor plumbing- one bathroom for the entire family but most were grown up by that time. When I was young, a bathroom was put downstairs because my grandparents were aging. It was near the music room that had a piano in it-between the parlor and the living room, there was a long narrow room where they put a small bathroom in one corner. The rooms were heated by fireplace or stove. They didn't use a lot of the house except for sleeping. We'd run upstairs in the freezing cold.

My lovely dollhouse! My oldest aunt, Eva, my dad's sister, married a carpenter. They lived across the street from my grandmother's in the valley and he built many homes in that area. There were stone and there were wooden homes. One year, my Aunt Nellie, the lawyer, thought we should have a doll house. We had a wealthy cousin who lived in Long Island...Richard Childs. She said, "Why don't you buy some furniture for the dollhouse we're making?" So, he went to F.A.O. Schwartz and he brought back living room furniture and two chairs with rush-bottom seats I recall the 3 pieces cost $17.50! My parents were horrified because their own living room furniture cost them $6. And here we had furniture for the dollhouse that cost so much! The year was 1928. My own children and grandchildren played with the dollhouse. It got damaged as we put it up to the attic. When I married, I didn't want to play with it or take it with me when we moved to Wallkill. So, it was put up into the attic. When my children were younger, I brought it home and we re-wallpapered a few rooms because the attic window had been left open and the wallpaper was stained. But nothing else was damaged. My children loved it and my grandchildren did, too. But they didn't play with it until they were older. They had to play with the furniture IN the house and not on the floor. However, they did put the furniture on the floor and someone stepped on it. So, I had to re-glue it.

When I was young, we ice skated on the stream right by our house. The Chestnut stream came right through Grahamsville and down through the valley and into the reservoir. We lived on the south side of Chestnut, so we went across foot bridges to my grandmother's house. We'd go past the barns on the road to Aunt Eva's house. Uncle Willis and Aunt Nellie took two orange crates. He built a roof and a porch on the end n this dollhouse. He did the carpentry work while my aunt wallpapered it. They made rugs and what they could to furnish it. Cousin Dick from Long Island found a club chair for it. It was $6.50 for that little chair by the fireplace. It now has a few added items because my friends wanted to bring me things when I moved here after 50 years. I told them that I didn't want a thing and I have all I need. So, they bought me a small hassock and kitchen items for that dollhouse.

We children really didn't work on the farm because the workers were afraid the horses would kick us. We went to the barn with an adult to see things but we didn't really work in the barn. We had one ugly horse The kids were scared to death of him. We had fresh milk and smoked meats. The farm worker's grandchildren who had been left orphaned worked on the farm.

People would do quilting in the living room. They used old clothes. Down was used for filler. Sometimes blankets were pieced together- nothing was wasted. All I've made, I've given to my children.

My grandmother who lived on the main road saw hoboes. They'd come up what is now Rt. 55 that led through the valley. They'd come to her door but they had to remain on her porch. They were kind and she would give them food. I recall seeing one with a stick and bandana, which held his belongings, slung over his shoulder. He sat on the porch steps and grandmother brought food to him. She didn't worry about being hurt. She just did NOT invite him inside.

Gypsies would come through once in a while. They were not invited in the house either. They would come into the store and some would have on big skirts. They'd leave with items hidden in the skirts. They just lived that way. When I stayed alone at the store my father would say, "If you see a car pull up and all these people pile out, lock the doors at once and do not let them in. You won't be able to watch all of them at once."

For entertainment, I went to the Rivoli theater. We had some choices where to go. Ellenville had Shadowland. In Monticello, there were 2 movie theaters. Liberty had a theater. I really didn't attend many movies until I was in my teens. I graduated from high school in 1938, a bit earlier was when I started to date. I was so young my folks wouldn't let me go out alone. My older sister and her boyfriend would go, too. There were all good movies in those days. I hardly go to a movie now. We'd go to these theaters on Saturday nights.

For entertainment, we stayed home with the family. I played the violin. Mom and my sister would play the piano. We played mouth organs and banjos. People gather around the piano to sing. We loved to play Parcheesi and other board games. I still have them! We played lots of outdoor games. We played baseball and used trees for bases. We really had no equipment. My children did the same. We didn't have a TV when my kids were young. I'm glad we didn't as we sat around together and played board games and also played outdoors. I think it was much better for them. We walked on home-made stilts. My sister would only get on them when she could stand on a big rock. We'd chase each other around on these stilts and have a great time. We pretended a lot. The big rocks were our store and the stones, our money. We had such great times using our imaginations. It seems that kids don't pretend anymore.

When I was the lead in the senior play in Ellenville, I was a mousy little girl. They needed a mousy character. The play was "The Poor Nut," by O'Neill. My dad couldn't afford to drive back and forth, so I boarded at the age of 15. My mother had stayed at the same home when she went to high school. Mrs. VanderLyn looked out or my mother when she was there and looked out for me also. She had a three-story house and would take in lodgers who worked on the dam or in the bank. I got a little room up in the attic. I walked to rehearsals and then she would feed us.

Since then, they've torn down the old brick school building where they had all grades. I graduated in 1938. Children were usually respectful. I was bored in grade school because I was listening to other classes; I talked a lot. I walked 2 ½ miles home once a week from the library in Grahamsville. Once a week I'd take out 7 books and would take them to school to read.

In those days, there were no guidance counselors. I was 15 and I knew what I did NOT want to be. I did not want to be a secretary and go to Poughkeepsie Business School. I did not want to be a nurse. They took their training right in the hospitals then. I did NOT want to be a teacher and go to New Paltz. I ended up doing this anyway. Those were the professions offered to girls!

My Aunt Nellie became a lawyer! Her folks told her that she could NOT be a lawyer; she HAD to teach school! She taught for 6 months in a little one room schoolhouse in Sundown. She went home to tell her parents, "I'm not going back! I am smaller than the kids. I will NOT go back and I'd rather scrub floors for the rest of my life! "So, she went to Monticello to John Lyons who was a well-known lawyer and asked if she could be a clerk in his office and study law under him! He was delighted. She read the law books and passed the NYS Bar without having to go to college.

Here is the advice I would give young people today. For one thing, do not throw everything out like people do today! I wash out plastic bags and reuse them. If anything gets a little rip, I mend it right way. I don't sew like I used to but I would never give up my sewing machine. I recently had a top on that was made ages ago because I took care of it. My niece exclaimed, "Aunt Margaret, you've still got one of these tee shirts made in Youngsville back in the 80's!" We took care of things! We didn't waste food and you were to finish what was on your plate! You fixed what needed repair. You put a new handle on the axe when needed it.

My primary household chore was dusting furniture. I hated this! My mother had Victorian furniture. My older sister got to use the sweeper and shake rugs. We had water from the spring that was piped down under the roads to my grandmother's house, to my aunt's and then to ours. It never went dry. A hot water heater was connected to the range and there was a nice sink. There was a bathroom upstairs. My parents had added on a sewing room and an enlarged living room with fireplace and window seats. Their bedroom was upstairs. We had 4 bedrooms but just one bathroom. My mother made all of our clothes. I never saw a new coat until I was in college in Greensboro, NC. Mom came down with my sister for Easter and said that I needed a spring coat. Previously, she'd rip up an old coat and replace the lining. She would make suits with her treadle machine. I made all my children's clothes, too. I mainly like to sew; you can get things finished in a hurry when you sew.

I had gone to Quaker boarding school one year and a Quaker College for two years. Maybe that was the result of the Depression. My father and his family were Quakers. In the former days, they wore dark clothes and bonnets. Three of the 10 children married Quakers. The older 5 went to Chappaqua for high school where there was a Quaker school. They couldn't go to school anywhere else unless they boarded. Yes, some spoke 'thee" and "thou."

My mom was Methodist. I thought I wanted to join the Methodist Church but my folks wanted me to wait until I was 18 to decide. They told me not to join a church just because my friends were there. When I turned 18, I wanted to be a Quaker!

My sister went to the George School, PA, a Quaker school, boarding for 3 years because they wanted her to have the Quaker experience. Dad's four siblings had gone here. When the Depression came, they were sorry that they could not afford to send me but for one year. When I attended a Quaker college- Guilford College in NC, it cost me $10 a month because I lived in a co-operative dorm. All 80 girls did all the work- cooking, cleaning, emptying the furnaces, and more cleaning. Tuition was $330. My older sister who had then gotten through Barnard College, paid my tuition. My cousin who worked in a Monticello bank would give me $5 a month for spending money. I had no trouble living on $5 a month!

Mother canned all kinds of fruits, vegetables, pickles and jellies. After I married, I would put up hundreds of quarts each year. At the farm, we had a cold storage place for apples and vegetables. This cellar was concrete and built on a bank; we had no refrigerator and kept milk down there. We finally did get an ice box; that was a big step! We would cut ice from ponds in winter and put it in. The ice was buried under sawdust. When we wanted to get ice for the ice box in summer, or make ice cream, we'd take those huge tongs, get the ice, put it in the wagon and bring it to the house.

We had a large pond which was right on the border of Sullivan and Ulster continues. You'd go down the road to the "County Line Pond." One night they'd been cutting ice on one end of the pond. There were no lights then. A couple of the fellas skated right off into the area where they were cutting the ice, and fell in the icy water. Near tragedy! All were careful after that. We'd congregate there in the winter and in the summer, it was our swimming hole. My dad was a wonderful skater! We'd make a huge bonfire to get warm. I don't recall ever seeing a snow plow.

In the 30's here, most people were farmers or had stores in Grahamsville. There were two garages in Eureka. There was a saw mill. The Chestnut stream was a nice level stream under the car bridge right by our house which was never more than 3 feet deep. On summer days, mother took us there. She never learned to swim. My cousin would be with us because her mother was ill in the Middletown Hospital.

The Dam - The State took over the land, eminent-domain. People from New York put up signs on all our buildings. All residents had to move out as that was where they were to put the dam. Then the war came along in '41. They hadn't finished the dam. Huge equipment had been brought in to make airfields, etc. Everything stopped. The dam was not completed until 1950 and that was when they began to fill it. We were the last ones to leave the valley because dad was the postmaster in Eureka, the last village.

During the Depression, there was little business at the store. Everyone had moved. Many moved to Kingston. They were not happy people as their ancestors had lived there for ages. My folks were sensible and bought a house on the Sundown Rd, 5 miles away. My aunts built on the Woodbourne Road, about 6 miles from where they had lived. They could all go the same church. My dad was on the Little World's Fair Board, the Cemetery Association and in the Odd Fellows. Mother was still in the Methodist Church. Then, it wasn't like people today who need to move because they take different jobs.

Today, people do not have those roots that their parents and grandparents laid down. Our relatives settled in this valley in the early 1800's. Erastus Smith Name was my great-great grandfather who settled in Eureka. These men named the village and the little store. Stamps were 2 cents. All would congregate in our store on rainy days to play dominoes. I loved being in the store to overhear these colorful folks.

A Quaker cousin - Willis Ryan- was a conscientious objector. He was in the Civilian Conservation Corps (CCC) or alternate service.

I married my high school sweetheart in 1941. Most people had moved out of the valley. We had an outdoor Quaker wedding. Workers on the dam were living in rooms at my grandmother's house. All watched.

We would all gather around the radio. Our very first radio had a big horn on its side. "The Myrt and Marge" show came on before supper time. We all wanted to rush home to listen to this program. Many people listened to record players. Another uncle who had two boys looked after us sometimes. They had a wind-up Victrola.

I think dad received about $800 a year as postmaster. Once the other families moved away, it was just this little store. As surveyors, dad and his father became well-known in this area. Those who went away and returned with college degrees would ask to find little corners in this area where they could live. Finally, dad was told that he needed a license. They helped him get the license.

Folks who had livestock in the valley would turn out their animals in the summer and not bring them back to the barn until winter. People built stone walls and fences when they cleared the fields.

A while later, my grandmother's family- the Reynolds- took in many boarders. People would bring up their children to go to summer camps here. Parents stayed at various boarding houses while visiting their children weekends. My mother thought that she, too, would take in boarders. We had 4 bedrooms. The girls slept in the woodshed. Harriet and I went to our playhouse to sleep. The boarders got first choice. There were no problems, though. We managed even with the one bathroom. They all got a fine breakfast the next morning. One boarder with whom we stayed in touch - the Spitzes - gave me a lovely wedding present the day I was married.

We picked rhubarb and vegetables as we needed. The boarders brought in needed money. There was no big deal made it of it, but the boarders brought in more than the $800 that dad made at the post office. Many visitors came by train from New York City to Ellenville and Fallsburg. Later, they drove big cars.

Each spring, we would go to New York City when there was a yearly Quaker meeting. It was in the 14th Street area. We stayed at the Friends' Seminary Quaker School while they were away on spring vacation. Dad made sure that we got to see loads of NYC sites when we would gather for this yearly meeting. I recall the Empire State Building and Chinatown in the 30's especially. I couldn't wait to get back home, though. In later years, we'd go to Radio City and to see plays on Broadway. Staying for the day was grand, but I loved returning home. My sister lived there so she was comfortable with the trains. No living there for me! Many school children in Ellenville arrived there by train. They came from Summitville, Phillipsport and Spring Glen. The train went through all those little towns.

Earlier, I mentioned conveyances. These were trucks...bread trucks and wagons...any type of transport as there were no busses for elementary school kids. They would bid to transport the children to school. We'd get in the two back doors and sit along the sides. My older sister had gone to Grahamsville School by sleigh.

In winter, we would have buckwheat pancakes. We'd stir up the batter like we would sourdough. We made our own bacon and sausages that went along with the farm-fresh eggs. We'd fry up the sausages and put them in cans and add some fat. The cans were turned upside down and that fat would seal the cans. That way, the meat wouldn't spoil. The cans would then go downstairs where it was cold. We'd get a can of sausage whenever we wanted it. The eggs were put down cellar in a "water glass." The liquid would seal the shells of the eggs. It was the coldest job! You'd put it all in a big crock. It was so cold that when you went to get the eggs with your hands, it was ice but that liquid did not freeze; it preserved those eggs.

My parents bought Harriet and me nice dolls. The outfits were made by my mother. We had our dolls, "POLLY PEPPER" and "PHRONSIE PEPPER" .... named for the Five Little Peppers book series! Every year, mother would have them dressed in new outfits that she had made. We didn't want any new dolls. Each Christmas morning, we couldn't wait to see our new doll outfits. I did the same with my girls when they were young. I dressed them - sometimes it would be a nighty and housecoat...sometimes a coat and hat...or a fancy bonnet and dress. Those Christmases were wonderful! My older sister never wanted to play with dolls. She liked school. That's why I was such a nuisance in school because I had already read all HER books. We'd "play school" and she was the teacher everyday once she got home from school. So, when I went to school, the teacher was dumbfounded as I already had read those books and knew the material.

We had a family dog at my grandmother's house. It went from one home to another to beg. But, he always knew when it was time to come home. The door would fly open but mother never allowed him inside. By the time I went away to school, someone had given us a kitten that was welcomed in the house. "Sambo" was thought to be a boy until it had kittens.

My folks had an ugly goose. Mother said not to take your eyes off him as he would nip your heels. One day Mother was crossing the footbridge and the goose was charging at her. She got so mad that she kicked it and killed it.

When chickens were killed, we'd put them in boiling water to pluck off their feathers. Then a flame burned off the pin feathers. Mother and dad, and later- my sister-in- law did all the cleaning. The first time I did it, I made such a mess with all the internal organs. They didn't want me to do that again!

Mother and dad never discussed the disadvantaged people of the 30's with us. They gave certain items to families in need. People did not toss away anything that could be re-used. We inherited shoes from the older person. Hand-me-downs were usual. They were mended and taken care of. We wore aprons to keep our clothes clean.

We girls never wore pants. In winter, we'd wear long wooly stockings fastened with garters. We wore long underwear under those. We were well-protected from the snow.

Winter meant tobogganing in the snow. We'd also ski. The skis had no fasteners; you'd just slip your feet through straps. When we went to my cousins for a weekend, we'd ski from here to Grahamsville which was about 4 miles. It was another 2-3 miles off Big Hollow Rd. to their place. I don't know how the straps stayed on. The next day, we'd ski some more. We roller-skated on my porch in Eureka. The skates were the kind you'd clamp on to the edges of your shoes and tighten with a key. My cousin, who had been to Syracuse, brought these back and we, too, learned to ski and roller skate.

My hair was always in a Buster Brown do. My dad would cut our hair. My sister, Harriet, cried so that he took her to the store and placed her up on a nail peg while the men were sitting around. He said, "Now- fuss if you want!" It was a while before I got a perm in a beauty shop.

Plays were presented at the Odd Fellows Hall. The building has a small stage at one end. In those days, many churches did not have spaces for gatherings, so they used the hall, too. Dances were held there. They'd have minstrel shows- where they'd blacken their faces. I recall getting in a fight over a chair with Billy. Our parents had to settle that fight. I was a bad egg.

The Little World's Fair has been there for a long time. I joined the 4-H when I was young - they had just started up. My great-grandfather and grandfather gave the first lumber to the fairgrounds. The hemlock was cut in their own sawmill. They also gave the first lumber to Grahamsville firehouse (which was torn down a few years ago). When they were demolishing it, I asked if I could have a piece of it. So, I took a huge piece with nails in it. I took it up to the new town hall where they brought in old-fashioned tools etc. and a big deal was made of this. The building says 1878 on the roof.

My relatives lived into their 90's. All were buried from home - laid out in the parlor. Quakers had no service as they do in funeral parlors. You sat in silence and read from The Bible. Just family and friends came. In Quaker meetings, the elders sat apart on facing benches. We all sat around a stove and families sat together. Because of the dam, the "home" cemeteries had to be moved. The workers were very respectful as every grave was moved.

Telephones - A long ring or a short ring- or 2 short rings. We didn't have one on this side of the stream as there were no lines. There was one at the store and one at my grandmother's. There was an exchange at Charlie Curry's Hardware Store in Grahamsville when you wanted to call outside this local area. I guess there was a switchboard. They lived upstairs. When it would ring, they'd have to run downstairs and switch it over.

My dad rigged an old phone so that we could call over to grandmother's. I would not talk on the phones as I had a hearing loss. I'd be told to pick it up when ringing and put it to my left ear but I would say I couldn't hear it! One day I put it to my right ear and I could hear! I was 10 or 11 and never knew I couldn't hear out of my left ear! I had compensated. I had had a bad ear infection when I was 9 or so and I didn't get back to school. Mother took me to a specialist. The ear was irrigated from March to August. At that time, I got the German Measles and Mumps at the same time. there was nerve damage.

Mother was a nurse and she'd be careful when we went to the dentist in Ellenville. I had these eye teeth (aka "fangs") and I was so self- conscious about them. I had one out. It was Regents time at high school. They said I'd need to come back another time to get the other one out. But- I was determined! At noon, between 2 Regents tests- I went to the dentist. He took out the other one behind it and I returned to the Regents! At dinner, I tried not to let my folks see, but someone said something funny. I laughed and they remarked, "You had the other one out!" My sister was strong-minded, too! She would clamp her mouth shut and refuse to go to the dentist. Later, she had to have a lot more work done on her teeth!

My mom painted all of these paintings. (Note: When did she ever had time for this?? They are VERY lovely!) While in her teens, she took art lessons from someone in Woodbourne. In her 70's, she painted while taking Adult Ed. Manville Wakefield bought the Reynolds house. He taught her art and told her to keep her own style. Her paintings are now in an art gallery.

I had 13 nicknames! I NEVER liked Peggy, or Maggie, or Mag. Margie was ok. Harriet had some horrid nicknames. I believe my name was from a make-believe playmate my sister had before I was born. I had a happy childhood- an excellent foundation!

The afternoon sped by so quickly...Margaret...not Peggy...is a spunky, enjoyable lady! A strong-minded individual!

Interview with Lester Huebsch, January 7, 2007 at Rock Hill Methodist Church. DOB 3/12/31.

Lester's family of 3 and 5 sisters lived in Liberty, NY near Zelkin's Junk Yard! The kids all walked to school which was about 1 mile away. In school, no one recognized that Lester had a severe hearing loss. The teachers talked very fast and Lester couldn't keep up with them and did not do well in school. [Later, Lester was tested and they discovered a severe hearing loss, possibly at birth.] However, he was a whiz at geography.

One early chore Lester recalls was picking berries. Summers, he and his sisters would pick berries (raspberries, huckleberries) and sell them to Yasgur's Farm for 10 cents a quart.

Because shoes were so expensive, most children went barefoot in the summer. My sister and I would race over cinders. Shoes were saved for school and special occasions. He recalls eating many pancakes and oatmeal as a youngster. Lester wore knickers for most of his childhood years. The whole family played board games, especially Monopoly. He and his siblings played loads of baseball. A treat was buying a Babe Ruth candy bar for 5 cents. For 30 cents, an entire afternoon could be spent at the movies (Liberty Theater) including a trip to the concession stand. His dad had a pick-up truck and all the kids sat in the back. His mom died at age 37.

We never saw a Christmas tree on that eve, but by the next morning there was a tree all decorated. My father had chopped down that tree from back in the woods. We each had very few gifts. Mostly we got shirts and socks. These were costly store bought. We were never excited about these gifts. The girls made rugs out of old shirts and dresses. We boys were constantly getting in fights 'til dad broke up these fights.

At age 16, Lester was accepted into the Civilian Conservation Corps (CCC) and was sent to California [The CCC was the brainchild of FDR whereby thousands of young boys would learn trade skills, perform emergency operations such as fill in creek beds and help preserve our nation's heritage. The CCC reforested thousands of acres of land, built park roads, erected dams and bridges, restored and preserved historic sites and fought forest fires nationwide. Boys served for 6 months but could reassign for up to 2 years.]

Lester recalls riding a troop train to Fallon, California. Here he learned various trades. His first training that first year was about the gypsy moth. He refers to his work as "Bug Hunting Camp!" When at Peekskill, NY, their job was to clear out the gypsy moth that devastated foliage. He learned carpentry in the CCC. Another job was clearing land for the Shasta Dam. He recalls that this task was done in 15 days of continual hard rain! RIP RAFTING ROCKS- they built rock sides for irrigation purposes. In Fallon, he laid concrete pipes. Lester completed his high school education while serving in the CCC. For his work, Lester recalls being paid $30 a month; $22 was always sent home. He felt a great need to help his father.

Lester joined the Army in WW II. Lester was married in 1942, while he was in the Army, he traveled to Africa where he drove a truck. He was not able to see his first-born daughter while he was away. He carried a photo of her in his truck. He later became a carpenter and built his own house. All helped each other with work then and still do to this day.

After some conversations, illnesses were mentioned. Lester evidently did not get the cancer genes that afflicted his family. On his father's side, they all died young. Lester felt that he may not live long, therefore he drew an early Social Security at age 62. Lester feels that his brother picked up the good genes, too. One sister is 99. Now at the age of 86, he misses getting the $44 a month more if he had waited til 65!

This marvelous, chipper man graciously allowed me to take his photo. What a charmer!

Interview with Pearl Dumont at Rock Hill Methodist Church, January 14, 2007. DOB 8/6/1927.

During the Depression years, we lived in Walden, NY. My father was working for a farmer so we had all the milk, cream and eggs we needed. My mother was at home. There was an Italian family near us that had a farm. My mother could help that family do their canning. They would can chicken, fruits and vegetables. My mother would bring home these canned items.

My father had his own business until the Depression hit and then all went downhill. We had a small house. It was very sparsely furnished. My mother was not a clutter bug and they bought only what was absolutely necessary.

My brother was 11 years older than I. He quit school and joined the CCC. He did 2 years of high school. Eventually my father met a man at Wanaksink Lake. They were in dire need of a caretaker and they liked each other. He got the job. We moved to Rock Hill. The house was not well heated but we kept the heat low anyway as it was costly. Father got a small salary and the use of the house. We didn't throw away money even if the heat was covered by the landlord! My father did handy work for wealthy people who lived along the Lake Wanaksink. He was a good electrician and did all sorts of handy work. My mother stayed home and was the in-between and watched houses while the owners were away.

I recall that we ate a lot of meatloaf. We had a friend who was a butcher. We were given lots of calves' liver. At that time, people were not thrilled to eat liver. My brother and I would pass this meat between us and the dog would be in between; the dog ate well. We ate all of what my mother canned.

Next to us was a field of blueberries. We had permission to pick these. We made blueberry wine. My parents were friends with the so-called "upper class people," who summered on the lake. There were always cocktails served. The house was in Pine Bush, I learned later, was sold to two Bohemian brothers. It was found out that these two were bootleggers. That's where the booze came from. When entertaining, you had to entertain back. They all drank this bootlegged stuff. When I was a little kid, I wasn't sure what they were doing but they DID drink a lot of this swill!

The one room school house early on had a 2 holer, outdoor privy. Dot Breen, her husband, Bob and brother-in-law, Dick and I would walk to school. Sometimes someone would pick us up in a car after school.

The bungalow people (roads were not plowed then so people only visited their bungalows in the summer!) would give my mother nice clothes for us.

I recall my teacher, Miss Denton. When my own son started school, the school was now housed in the church building. (Now the Rock Hill Methodist Church) His teacher was Miss Denton also! Another teacher I fondly recall had long blonde hair. I was teacher's favorite then. I may have been her pet. At lunch time, she would take down her hair and comb it. I loved her hair! She was very strict. She would beat the boys…one in particular. She had a rubber hose. She would miss and hit the wall and we would be listening and all cringe.

At home my chores were helping with the laundry and the cleaning. I would dust and my mother would do the floors. Each spring was cleaning time. We started at one end of the house and never stopped 'til we reached the end! I recall the dandelion salad that we ate a lot.

Fun was ice skating. The Breen boys lived across the street. Where the hill is now, the old road that led to Wurtsboro, there was a house that is now falling apart. There was a long hill where we sledded. We would ice skate on a small pond near there. At the lake, we took swimming lessons and played ping pong there.

The first movie I recall vividly was "Snow White and the Seven Dwarfs." I remember my brother, Ted, complaining that it was not his cup of tea. He laughed more than I did. The theater was in Middletown. There was lots of penny candy-good sized. Milky Ways and Hershey bars were 5 cents.

Down from where I lived there was a general store called Brundages. There was a bar there and they sold groceries. I was one of the rug-rats who constantly ran in and out of there. People bought on credit but not MY parents! If they couldn't afford it, they did not get it! That certainly rubbed off on me. If we NEEDED something, we saved for it.

At this store, there was a slot machine- a one-armed bandit. There were no laws back then. Every once in a while, I would get a nickel. I would waste it on that machine. I never won a thing! I would kick myself in the pants but kept on trying! Ice cream or candy would have been 5 cents.

Regarding a favorite song...I can't carry a tune in a bushel basket. Before I was married, I saw so many Broadway plays. But, as far as having a favorite song, I can't recall. I used to do a lot of reading. I recall a program on the radio. Father Collier preached. He preached what might be called "leftist" material. Sunday afternoon, the rest of us would clear out of the house. What fascinated my father I don't know. Maybe it was because the preacher brought up issues that were not talked about in a small town. I listened to "The Lone Ranger," "The Green Hornet", "The Shadow," and "Jack Armstrong". We all gathered around the radio to listen. My kids didn't believe I didn't have a "box" to watch, just the radio. I was dirt-poor but my parents were self-sufficient. They never asked anyone for anything. Our family was always willing to help anyone if we could. And they lived in the limits of their income.

My favorite toy was my dollhouse. I guess it was a very bad year when I received it and before my brother, Ted, went to the CCC. He and my father built me a dollhouse. My mother did the sewing...little rugs, curtains, and some home-made furniture. It was so beautiful! I do not know what happened to it. I recall my absolute joy that Christmas morn!

Looking back- sometimes can be good; At other times, not! I recall when I went to school over there (She points to a building across the street). It was a one room schoolhouse then. Every year Santa Claus visited us. Monticello undertakers always sent down oranges for us. You know the small boxes animal crackers came in? These small boxes contained Christmas candies.

Each kid got one. We looked forward to it so. The orange and the candies were real treats in our stockings. I didn't get coal but my son got some!!

I wore home-made dresses and they were nice. I have a photo of one dress. For a Christmas play, I had a dress of velveteen and fur. My mother redesigned the whole beautiful dress. My mother must have scraped for money and I didn't have to worry about shoes and clothes. My mother was "hot to trot" in NYC when she shopped. There were many thrift shops.

I had real reddish-brown thick curly hair. Even when I was young, I was never one for makeup. Dot (Breen) and I went to Sunday school here in Rock Hill. I recall that my mother wore earrings and always wore lipstick. She wouldn't go out unless she had on lipstick.

My father died when I was 16. He was a civilian employee for the Army. We had moved to Alabama and Georgia. I quit high school in my second year. When my father died in Alabama, they had to hold his body a whole year in case he owed any money. Figure out that one! Debts had to be settled! My mother brought dad home a year later and he was buried. We stayed in NYC then. My brother and father had built a house on Wanaksink Lake which sat empty for about 3 years. My mother and I returned to NY. We had no insurance or anything. We then lived in a small brown-stone house in an area called Railroad Flats.

I went to work for the Mana Electric job. I'd spray the heaters. I was the only girl and was spoiled rotten by the makes that worked there. When I began a task, they would then take over. Then, I went to work for the telephone company. That was boring. I was a telephone operator. A friend next to me was very well endowed. At that time, we talked directly to customers. We had tickets which we wrote out when a customer wasn't too nice. She had more tickets in her cleavage!

Then I met Mr. Right! I was married in 1947. I was only married 16 years. He had rheumatic fever when he was in the Navy. We stayed in central NY. My daughter was 8; my son 13 when my husband passed away. Fortunately, my mother loved my husband. My father-in-law always called me "Miss Pearl." My husband Paul's dying wish was to see that our kids had a better education than we did. There would be money from Social Security and some from the Army. I worked. I set aside to accounts- one for Donna and the other for Paul Stephen. I could have stayed home to collect Social Security, but I worked part-time in the post office. I also worked at the diner in Rock Hill. I also worked at a French restaurant in Wurtsboro. I worked three jobs. Both my kids got their Masters!

My husband (and I'd do it all over again as he was such a wonderful man!) said to me," If you had pierced ears, I'd get you diamond earrings for Christmas!" He came home the next day and Pearl had her ears pierced. You didn't go to a barber shop to get the piercing done. I had called my doctor in Monticello. I asked, "Dr. Hornblum, do you pierce ears? If I get my ears pierced, Paul will buy me diamond earrings!" He replied, "At least you will pay me. I did my wife's ears, and she paid nothing!" I did get those earrings! He and my mother went to NYC and bought them in a pawn shop. God knows what he paid for them They're now in a velvet bag; I hardly ever wear them now. I've given my daughter most of my jewelry.

I don't recall FDR being elected. I recall the speech he made on Pearl Harbor Day...the day of infamy. My mother was in the hospital quite sick. I walked into her room and she was shushing me. I went over to her bed and she whispered," President Roosevelt died!" I asked why we were whispering. She said that the girl next to her in that room was hysterical over his death.

My grandmother who was 96 when she passed had a portrait of FDR hanging in the hallway. She worshipped my brother and he could do no wrong. When she would suggest something to him, he would "yes her to death" and then go do what he wanted to anyway. She attended my wedding but she did not stay for the reception as she was mad at me. Anyway, she had this picture of FDR. Ted would flip over the picture every so often and I would get blamed for it! Again, Ted could do no wrong! The radio Fireside chats were valued. Everyone listened. To me, the president deserves respect...much the same as minister or a teacher. I know my parents were Republicans. Often you're born into a religion and political party. These chats were extremely informative. There wasn't much other type of communication then. He would cover all that happened during the week. At age 11, these were fascinating to hear.

Pearl's mother was a disciplinarian. She was the one who would swat when someone needed to be kept in line. Her dad, who wore glasses, only had to look over the rims of the glasses at her and the she knew something was wrong. Dad always had his car and a pack of camels. He was content with those!

I recall seeing the food lines in NYC. Mostly men were in those food lines. Some women were there, too. Women then weren't as brazen as they are now.

The advice I'd give young people today? Remember that there is going to be a tomorrow and, another tomorrow. Nothing comes free and you must work for it and be accountable. Those are my personal feelings. Nothing is just handed to you. What I have, I've WORKED for. Even with my lack of higher education, I became a postmaster in Loch Sheldrake. With my brother's lack of education, he became a supervisor with the US Customs Office. He has letters from President Eisenhower who had fallen aboard ship. Ted and the medical staff were waiting for him when the ship docked. You aim for what you want even if it is WORK to get there.

I was very sick last spring. My daughter gave me a compliment saying, "You know, mom. You were 10 times sicker than this other woman in the room. She was being such a "wuss' with her illness. You are recuperating rapidly because you ARE a PUSHER." I did not want that walker or a cane.

My children thought they could help by paying for a cleaning lady every couple of months. I said, "It is Pearl cleaned!!" At my age, I can't move furniture. When my son-in-law visits, I get him to move the furniture and then I spot clean. I am now forbidden to go downstairs as the steps are steep and dangerous. (Of course, occasionally I DO walk down here! That's ME!)

I did work with the Ambulance Corps. I am still an auxiliary member. I run their penny socials. My grandson is now 21. From his 1st to 5th grades, I volunteered in his class.

Today in church I asked us to pray for Mrs. Barrish, a teacher he loved. I received a Christmas card from her saying, "May we mentally dance in the snow this winter." A beautiful memory.

My daughter now teaches in Cooke Middle School. After my grandson, Paul, went to middle school, I returned to Susan Dallache's 2nd grade class to volunteer. She retired 2 years ago and for all that time I was a school volunteer. Loved it! I look at the booklets those kids made and I cry. I look at the drawings, the spelling. In my own grandson's booklet, it reads, "I want to be in the ambulance corps like my daddy. I also want to be a vet!" The teacher had given me this booklet. Phew! Anyway, he is now an EMT in Binghamton.

Pearl is a spunky lady who is exceedingly glib. We laughed and we had very serious moments during this interview.

Interview with Angie Pettaluga at her home, March 7, 2007 DOB 12/19/1919.

I was 10 in 1929 when the Depression started. I was born in Hazel, NY which is a little hamlet that had an acid factory in town. My father worked there because he had knowledge they needed in their work force. He was asked to move from Grooville, NY (near the Delaware border) to Hazel. The company gave little houses to those who worked there. That's where I was born. The job didn't last. Previously he had been a barber in the Delhi-Downsville area. He got a chance to move back down here to Monticello. Tom Depace had a barber shop on Broadway and asked him to work for him.

My mother had had a baby in Grooville and I came along 14 months later. She also had a 5-year-old daughter as my father had been married previously and the mother died.

We moved into an area that used to be called Washington Heights in Monticello, NY. It's now Rt. 42 going toward Pt. Jervis. We had a little bungalow behind Hamilton's big house. I remember that house vividly even though I was possibly 4 years old. The Hamilton boy slapped me. There was large rock nearby and we all wanted to lay on that rock. He slapped me and took over that rock.

Then we moved to Pelton's Farm. They had big places in Sackett Lake and Monticello. My father was to farm that land. My brother was born there. He still worked as a barber and was planning to get his own place.

The Pelton Farm started at the end of Park St. where there used to be a fairground. They had dog and horse racing at that county fair. Beyond it, was a small airport. The farm was above that and came all the way over to the road that goes to Pt. Jervis, Rt. 42 S. Years later, part of that farm became the County golf course.

I started school late because the school was on John's St. in front of the Court House My mother thought we were too little to walk that far so she kept my sister and me home until she was 8 and I, 7. School wasn't mandatory then. When we finally did start school, we walked 1 ½ miles. I recall wearing Arctic boots in the winter. They were galoshes with buckles that you had to close. I hated them!

Miss Marshall was my 3rd grade teacher. She held me back a year...maybe that's why I recall her. Myrtle Bell (Johnson) was my1st grade teacher. I don't recall the name of my 2nd grade teacher.

People in 1926/27 were always discussing the hard times they were in and more to come. The CRASH hadn't occurred yet.

The school I attended was torn down and the high school became the grade school. A new high school was built alongside where my elementary school was. There was a playground that had a 4-foot fence around it. We kids used to like to turn on it. You'd put your hands on the top of the fence and turn completely over around the steel fence. I recall that we were out for recess and Doris Tompkins had twirled around the fence and scraped her head on the ground and had a terrible brain injury. Her father was a photographer in town.

Mrs. Gallighan taught 8th grade geography. She came from the Otisville/Cutterback area. Her whole family was very involved in politics. She would line us up in separate boy/girl lines-tall to short. I didn't like that because was tall for my age, and I was first!

Restrooms with plumbing were in that school. We had a cafeteria. We did not have a gym. I was spoiled by my own mother's home cooking as she made her own bread and butter. We brought bag lunches. We mostly had maiden teachers- Miss Gallagher, Miss Shank, Miss. Osborne. Ken Rutherford was our principal. Mr. Fuller as our band teacher and I played trombone. We would get into games free by playing in the band. I recall that certain kids who acted up were made to sit at their desk in the hallway outside the classroom. Joe and Jerry DePaul were in the hallway a lot!

My brother, Ivan, loved all critters. He would roll up the bottom of his shirt as a holding area for snakes. He was paddled when be brought snakes into the classroom. One day an all-white horse was found in the high school gym. My brother was blamed for that. Whenever a kid acted out in school, he was sure to be punished more severely when he got home.

My sister, Ida, was the class valedictorian. She was very smart. I was always put up to her as I was only an average student.

At home, we had a huge garden. All the kids did chores. I recall taking two stones and scraping the potato bugs off the potato plants. It was the kids' chore to take these bugs off. There were no bug sprays then. It was usually dark when we walked home from the field. Many kids who walked home were from our area of Monticello called "Dog Town." I don't know why it was called that but it was across the tracks. This area used to have boarding houses for summer folks. There was a little store we walked past each day, Weizner's Store. We'd all walk there en route to Sunday School and church services. We loved the penny candy there. On Sundays, my father would give us pennies and nickels and we'd walk past the Presbyterian Church up by the Court House. On St. John's Street before you got to Broadway, there was a hotel. Here was Kennedy's Candy Store. We'd give the church the pennies and keep the nickels for the candy. I can remember holding a penny in my hand and dropping it in the collection. Kennedy got more money than the church did!

We had a teacher who lived in Hurleyville who taught us penmanship, the Palmer Method. I don't see good penmanship these days. We would practice loops and all until they were perfect. English is so important. Today we overhear all sorts of languages. Back then, we didn't have different language-speaking people.
One of the biggest changes was when the library building was built. I believe that was 1929. We HAD to be well-read.

In school, we were taught to bank our money. We would bring 5 cents and put in in our bank and have it entered in a bank book.

When I was in 2nd grade, we moved from the Pelton Farm to downhill to the back of the fair ground's entrance. Our house was right by the Park Ave. entrance. My mother had inherited some money and they bought the former Cantrel house. My father had a barn in the back. We had horses, cows and chickens. We collected eggs daily.

We kids got along marvelously. We thought up our own recreation. I'm not sure when Al Capone became popular. I was in grade school and we got ahold of a book about him. I recall that they called their women, "Molls." 'Cross the street from the house was a small ticket booth, an entranceway to the fair. When it wasn't active, it was a clubhouse for us kids. We had our own little Al Capone play-acting. We knew all their names and acted out stories. Ozzie Stanton from a well-to-do Monticello family was always Al Capone. Ozzie became a famous lawyer.

We would pick huckleberries and sell them for 10 cents a quart to the summer people. Movies were 10 cents. We'd go out early in the morning to pick so we would have money for the movie. I recall seeing "Midsummer Night's Dream," with Mickey Rooney. Even cabs were 10 cents.

For Christmas, we would get an orange and nuts. We loved getting the orange as a treat!

In school, milk cost 3 cents for a small carton. We even had chocolate milk. I recall when they sold us sour milk- no refunds there.

I recall the school nurse, Mrs. Harter, who was very mean.

Dr. Brady delivered my brother, Ivan, at the house. My sister had rheumatic fever and the doctor diagnosed her with Pleurosis. He took her to the hospital in his own car.

My mother was very clever. She would get various clothing from others and redesign them and make them over for us to wear. We never went without. Honestly, I don't know how she managed. She was constantly working. We had a huge garden and she would can everything.

From time to time, we would take in boarders. A friend of mine who was living in Minneapolis during the Depression had seen men standing in soup lines. They were given runny, weak soup. Men were on street corners selling pencils and apples for a nickel. I recall homeless people who pitched a tent in the woods here. They were the mother, father and 4 kids. Their chimney went right through the roof of the canvas.

My dad would sit at the table and dole out where the money would go. One pile was for the mortgage, the next for coal, the next pile for taxes, etc. Unfortunately, my dad was given to drink and that cause arguments. I worked in a laundry summers. I was in charge of pressing out the excess water from the clothes. In the summer, I would get so hot and sweaty working there. It paid poorly.

Black Friday was real! I recall that Dick Shevelle lost his whole fortune in 1929. We lived in his house, bought it from him and he continued to live there until his death,

Saturday nights were bath nights. We'd get washed in a huge galvanized tub. I don't recall shampoo. I'm sure we used a bar of soap for our hair.

I worked for the telephone company for 33 years. I gradually rose in status. At age 16, I was transferred to Florida, NY where I was chief operator. I was married at age 27 and had 5 children. I was always taking maternity leave! Then, I worked for the NY Telephone Company and earned $10 a week. The older I became, the younger the supervisors over me were. They were college people. I know I was singled out due to my gray hair. So, I dyed it! I was on my own. I remember betting money on races and losing it all! I learned from that!

When asked what advice, she would give to our youth today, Angie replied: We were taught to manage with what we had. Her mom would say: "Make do. Do over. Or, do without."

Interview with Lenny Moskowitz, January 18, 2007 DOB 1/5/26.

We lived on Saratoga Avenue, Brooklyn, NY. My father had a butcher shop. We had moved to the Brownsville area in Brooklyn. My father took a chance and borrowed money in order to open his shop.

One early vivid image I have...I was maybe 6 or 8.... was in the winter. The unemployed men would like up with the Works Progress Administration (WPA). They were given shovels for shoveling snow. I don't recall how much they were paid...maybe a dollar or two a day. They shoveled snow into drains on each corner when two streets intersected. I recall that they were so ill dressed- old overcoats, shoes, and seldom boots. Many had no gloves. They were poor men trying to earn something for the day. That imagine had remained with me all these years. I can still see them. The shovels were wide, maybe scoop shovels. I'm sure the WPA gave out the shovels. These were hard-working men; they were struggling. They could have been tailors out of work...who knows? They would pile the snow high up on the curbs. We kids would climb on these piles and make igloos. The huge heights of the snow mounds looked like a scene from Siberia.

I know when an emergency came up, my parents had to borrow money. They always paid it back in due time.

I distinctly remember the movie industry wanted to grab whatever it was...maybe 30 cents admission. Every Friday night they gave away a free dish. My mother would go see the actor she loved - her "Clarkie," she called him (...aka Clark Gable) We'd frequently go to the Supreme theater and she'd get her dish. When I got older, my father would take us to the Pitkin Theater. No matter what, we always sat in the loge which cost a wee bit more, but smoking was allowed. When you are a merchant and in the retail business, there's money around somewhere. You'd pay the slaughterhouse...next week.

I remember that I was coming home from school, PS 174...which was 2 long blocks away but on the other end of the block from where my father's store was, and I was walking on the opposite side of the street. That day the school had given us all little stickers to paste in our windows that read: "NRA" (National Recovery Act). Roosevelt had just gotten this Recovery Act going. Banks were closed. It was a sticker to promote his new society, The New Deal. So, they used the public-school kids to get stuff to their parents. As I was walking down the street, a kid ran by me (SOB!) and he grabbed the thing out of my hand.... ripped it right from my hand. I recall it had an eagle on it...it was blue. He took the whole thing or tore it in half then ran away. The Klutz! I ran crying to my father's store where my mother worked also. You know what a KLUTZ is? It is a big wooden butcher block. Today in Jewish when you speak of someone who is stupid and clumsy, you call him a "Klutz," probably from the German.

So, my mother worked every day and came home to cook dinner. The big invention then was the pressure cooker. It saved a little time. She was a very good cook. This was a Kosher butcher shop and people only ate the fore-quarters of a cow...not bone or sirloin. People would come for bones to make soup. We didn't sell chickens. The other half of the shop was rented to a "chicken man." The front part of this store was rented to a produce man. They were all able to share the rent.

On the block from us was Fortunoff's (for people from that area they will recall a store named Fortunoff's). It was started by a peddler. Today, it's a very famous store. It was a huge store on our block

The first day I went to school, I cried.

I had a little dog named Snowball.

Our family always had enough to eat. The difference between Gladys' [Lenny's wife] diet as a child and mine was that my father was a butcher so we had meat daily. Gladys' father peddled fruits and vegetables on the street for his living so they ate a lot of fruits. The whole dietary background was different.

As a child, to me, a couple of pennies was a lot of money. People didn't have their own telephones. So, across the street from us was a small candy store. They had a telephone. If you wanted to reach someone on that block, you'd call the candy store's number. The guy would come out and call the kids to go to Mrs. Schwartz's to say she had a call. You ran there and Mrs. Schwartz would give you a nickel. Kids would cluster around the candy store because no one had a phone. Those people made their living selling candy and seltzer.

Public school went to grade 6. I remember crossing the street from the school was a candy store where I'd go when school was out. He'd sell "Picks." It was a big board with little pieces of paper you'd punch out and if you had a winning number, you'd win. They would also contain baseball cards. If the candy was white, you'd get a penny candy; if it was pink, you'd get a larger candy bar. It cost a penny a pick. If there were no pinks left, we'd still try to win! People were making a living off penny sales.

In school, they had an "experimental" educational system for some children. You had the same teacher for 5 terms. I had Mrs. Speigel for my teacher. She was specially trained. These was just one Black kid in school. These were called "Activity Classes." We learned of Ben Franklin and made maps of the planets. These were ways to motivate the children. Therefore, when I completed those lessons and got out of that school to go to regular school, I had a tough time. I couldn't complete some lessons. They took away Mrs. Spiegel. The kids I sat next to would bribe me to give test answers. The kids would give me little lead soldiers which I collected. At an early age, I believed in "the free enterprise system." I recognized this as a marvelous system!

I recall the street peddlers with their little silver carts... There was a man who came by with little cart. There was burnt charcoal in the bottom and knishes on top. For 3 cents, you could buy a knish. I loved these! Gladys liked the sweet potato man who would come by and for 2 cents, you'd get one; for a nickel, you could get a potato the size of a Buick! I didn't like sweet potatoes! There was a man who sold Bubba Arbls..." Bubba" meaning "grandmother," and "Arbls" means chickpeas. For 2 cents, you'd get a small envelope and a big salt shaker. So delicious! With the knish, you'd get mustard or salt for 3 cents. People do not want to make penny sales these days! They want to outlaw the penny because It's costing the government more money to mint these than they are actually worth.

Gladys recalls roasting a "mickie," a potato! There was an empty lot in the neighborhood. All the kids got together and collected wood. The grocery man had wooden crates we used. You didn't use cheese boxes as these were very valuable! We waited 'til dark to start the fire. The kids would go home to get a potato. All had potatoes in their homes! You'd put the potato in the ashes and when cooked, take it out. These ashes are probably why they lived a long time! We don't know what chemicals and vitamins are IN the ashes! They were delicious even with the ashes! It was a social event for the kids. They would all get a "mickey" from home. When you speak to folks of this era, they will remember the "mickies."

I recall H.G. Wells and listening to "War of the Worlds". I was home alone in Brooklyn and was switching stations on the radio. I guess by the time I switched to that station and heard "This is a play" … who cared? I was scared!!!

In Brownsville, the Jewish gangsters (AKA "Murder Incorporated") killed for the Italian gangsters. They would go around collecting protection money from the merchants. One night my mother and father had to go out to meet a gangster who would help them get the gangs off their backs. My mother wouldn't let my father go alone. I had surmised this from their conversation. It was pitch black that night and they went off. I recall that mother had on a hat and my father was scared. (BTW-It wasn't until I was 26 that I realized that I could speak Yiddish! We travelled to Israel and it just came!!) My mother graduated from Woodridge High School and my father spoke with an accent; he did speak English and could read it. They'd switch to Yiddish when they didn't want this kid to know what they were saying. So, they went to meet the gangster who might get them off the hook and beg for mercy. They were to meet in the entrance of Fortunoff's, at the display window which was not easily seen from the street. People preyed on others there. "Murder Inc." was comprised of famous (infamous) Jewish gangs in the Brownsville area. I know I fell asleep that night and they put me to bed once they returned home.

Later when I went to junior high, a store opened up on Sutter Ave. All they sold was french fries! They cost a nickel. They'd give you salt and catsup. Another man would go around pushing a big baby carriage-like thing with a cake of ice. He sold snow cones. He'd have big tonic-like bottles with flavors. He'd scrape the shavings and toss on the flavor. (We saw one in Ellenville recently.)

My mother bought a newspaper each day. It was THE DAILY NEWS. The 3rd or 4th time Roosevelt ran, the newspaper didn't back him. My mother was furious; she never bought the NEWS again! She switched to THE POST- a bit more liberal. My mother was a staunch Democrat! The NEWS cost 2 cents and the POST, a nickel. Nevertheless, her principles would not let her by a paper that wouldn't support Roosevelt. Newsboys were on the corners. My mother had a picture of FDR in her kitchen. In later years, she placed a picture of JFK next to it.

She didn't know that FDR didn't want to help save the Jews in WW2! And all the Jews were his great supporters!

Kids and sometimes, men would shine shoes to make money.

Every year we would go to our wealthy Aunt Lena's home. Her husband owned hotels in NYC. He was a very elegant man and suave. He was a ladies' man. His speech as eloquent. She had 3 sons and a daughter. While I was there, they had a big, long table. One year, Wendell Willkie was running for President against FDR. I was around 14. They were all sitting around talking about voting. My cousin, Harold, announced that he was voting for a Republican! All were in shock! We had never heard of a nice Jewish by voting Republican! What an astonishing thing! Even the turkey on the table gasped for breath in awe.

I recall taking the train a few times and the hackney. My father didn't usually drive. He bought a little red roadster with a rumble seat. He'd leave at 5 a.m. to the slaughterhouse to pick up meat for the store. I only saw him drive that once. I guess he thought at that time of the morning, it was safer and he was not a good driver.

We didn't see many black people here. Each year my grandfather had a handyman. I was a little kid then. My grandmother had a small grocery store. I don't know how she ran that store so well because she hardly spoke English. They had a cow. This Black fellow named Algee, would have to go get the cow. He'd take me into the pasture and I got to ride the cow back. That was fun! There was another black fellow, named Mendel. He came around wearing a red beret and driving a big convertible. The woman with him may have been Creole. Folks were shocked because she passed for white. He performed in hotels. What was interesting was that he spoke impeccable Yiddish! He would sing in Yiddish. All loved to have him entertain.

We would swim under the old bridge in Woodbourne. They moved that bridge to where there were mazes of ducks. The workers came with a steam shovel and wrecked our swimming hole. They didn't have the dam yet. Maybe the WPA financed the start of the dam at that time.

My uncle had a one-armed bandit in his place. He would sell illegal alcohol during the Prohibition, of course, for medical purposes! An old farmer would come around at the back of the store. He'd take me upstairs to where there were 5 gallon drums. I'd take a hose to siphon it off but I never got it out of my mouth in time. It was 180 proof and it burned like hell! My mother would pick huckleberries and blackberries. We'd take a 5-gallon drum and put the berries in the bottom with a lot of sugar. Then he'd fill the rest with alcohol and take the drums back to the City. They were then put in closets!

Every year a man would pick apples in the apple orchard that my grandfather had. He'd then make cider. He'd give a certain portion back to the landowner. So, we always had cider in our home.

My grandfather would kill chickens for the butcher for a nickel a piece. It was a "penny-ante" living! This man would say, "You killed 60." Then my grandfather would counter with, "No. I killed more than that!" Everyone struggled to financially keep their heads above water.

Hotels had no luncheonettes that served ice cream and sandwiches. After the shows, most guests would go into town for refreshments. All the towns seemed to have these. Woodbourne had become a metropolis. My uncle would give a free ice cream soda to the member of the staff who brought in the crowd that night; usually the activities' director. Every hotel had their own performers...a Danny Kaye type of thing.

The movie theater was a hard luck one. I don't recall when it was built but it was elegant. During the difficult times, my uncle who bought a movie projector, would show movies in the back of his store. They were just starting talkies then. Maybe he charged 15 cents.

Everything came via train. We'd go into Fallsburg to get the big cartons of ice cream packed in dry ice. We needed to go in a couple of times a week. There weren't too many trucks making deliveries. Before the Depression, Old Rt. 17 went up the Wurtsboro Mountain and cars would turn around and go up backwards. They'd shift into rear gear as that was the strongest. Much of the traffic were Hackies. There were big cars with canvas that went over the isinglass and they'd transport people here. They had offices all over town and would really pack in those people. I recall that kids sat on an ironing board to pack them all in. Trains went to Fallsburg or Hurleyville train stations. We rode up here on the train a few times. I believe that people picked up the coal from the tracks. The train would come in on Friday. Then busses came in Fridays with all the husbands. That was known as "The Bull Train." All those bulls were coming here to do what bulls do...and it wasn't giving milk. Later, when the men came via bus on Fridays, it was the "Bull Bus." Many left on Mondays.

My mother was a very good cook. She had the finest meats to work with...such as kishka and stuffed derma. She'd take the cow's intestine and stuff it with flour and spices. They still sell this in delis. My wife couldn't believe that I could eat 4- 5 lamb chops at one sitting...baby lamb chops.

On Sunday mornings, I'd sleep late, maybe 'til 12 and I would have steak for my breakfast. When Gladys (wife) came to my house, my father would pick out the finest cuts of meat for her. When my daughter was born, he was so thrilled. For her first meat, he searched for the very best lamb chops.

I think things were not different until the 1940's. I was 14 in 1940. I worked at my uncle's drugstore lugging huge cases of soda upstairs. At the end of the summer, families would begin to leave. I wore knickers. They were always falling down around my knees. And, they were always worn at the knees. I played "tickets." You'd get a "ticket" with gum...a war scene or baseball player. You'd put 20 of these together with a rubber band. You'd toss them and the one who got closest to the line on the sidewalk won. With a bundle, you'd want to get it on the line. You got down on your knees to toss. My knicker's knees were always worn. My father took me to Stone Avenue to have 2 suits made. They were teal. I was 17 or 18 and the same size as my father. When I went out and my suit wasn't clean, I'd grab his! He was furious! He was a most meticulous man and didn't go out that often. I was his size for just one year. He was 5'11, weighed only 145 and he worked so hard.

I spent summers in Woodbourne, NY. My uncle had a drug store. This was in the 1940's. I worked for him as a stock boy and then graduated to "soda jerk," a soda dispenser! All the relatives worked for him. When I was little, my cousin and I would go to his store at night and take scoops and dig in the ice cream. He knew.

At the hotel, there were the nouveau riche; every woman had a fur, a mink stole. There were casinos. After the show in the nightclub, they'd rip off covers, and there were craps tables! The men stayed and shot craps. The sheriff would come and the owner would pay a certain amount of money for that gambling concession.

People stayed in boarding houses. You had a bedroom. The communal bathroom was down the hall. There was huge table where you ate with 20 other families. You weren't waited on. The kitchen was huge. They all shared that ice box. My grandfather who had a boarding house had an ice house. Uncle Henry, who was the youngest son, would have to go get the ice. There was the biggest coal stove I've ever seen- half as big as this room. Everyone wanted to be at the hot spot on cold nights. If a guest was cooking, another would come along and put her pot aside! In later years, they got two little refrigerators which two families shared. Also, later, small stoves were available for them. These were poorer people who welcomed a get away from the City. A room could be rented for $50 or $60 for the summer. They would bargain with my grandparents about the price.

There were itinerant performers who would go around and arrange little shows in the dining rooms. All the families would come. A woman would sing or there was a comedy act. I recall a woman who had a disfigurement in her mouth and she would blow out a candle. It was humorous to watch for this little kid. A guy would come to play his fiddle. Someone would sing, "My Yiddish Mama" and all would cry. This was part of the culture and socializing. Then, after the entertainment, they'd pass around a hat. At the end of the summer, families would begin to pack up and return home. They piled their stuff high in the hack. The ones remaining would bang on pots and pans as a sendoff. I guess the last one to leave would have had a silent departure!

In this home that had over 20 rooms, there were 3 bathrooms. There was a privy outdoors. My grandmother had a grocery store in the building. Oranges came wrapped in orange tissue paper. The lemons were wrapped in yellow tissue. I don't know about the peaches! So, they would cook in the communal kitchen and eat in the communal dining room. You can see that this could cause problems. People wanted the big bedroom in the corner of the house! My mother and father had a room at the top. Sometimes bedbugs were prevalent. They'd take mattresses outside and clean them with kerosene. It was a whole different culture.

We had "Bossy," the cow. NOT a Jewish name! My Uncle Henry had to go get her each morning and milk her. All the tenants wanted milk for their children. They were in the country where one could get this fresh milk. How much milk does a cow give? Maybe 2 gallons? There was never enough. My grandmother put water in the milk. In the end, it was very thin. She made delicious things even though she was not an excellent cook. She would take the skins of oranges and jelly them with sugar. They'd crystalize. She'd do this with lemons, too. You didn't throw away the peels. Delicious! You can still buy them as candies. There were always plenty of flies around in the kitchen and dining room. NO fan! There was always sticky fly paper around. All those folks were Jewish, so Kosher laws were observed.

The first time I went to a barber shop, I cried! I was frightened and hated it. I don't like anyone fussing with my hair. It cost 25 cents, I think. The day I was married, I got a shave from the barber. It was the only time I did that. Maybe it was custom. When my mother and father got engaged, my grandfather's duty was to take him to a Turkish bath...to look him over to see that he had all of his parts! This may have been a European custom. It was cheaper than getting a doctor's note! (my son-in provided me with this information.)

My mother's brother was a dentist. The family got his services for nothing!! He had lived with my mother for years and they had a close relationship. He was shaving once and his suspenders were just hanging. I was a wild little kid. I grabbed the suspenders and ran to the other side of the room and let them go. He cursed me out so! I had happy years in Woodbourne as a boy. There were a lot of kids around. I went swimming daily! My grandfather was a rabbi and my mother still let me go swimming even on Tisha B'Av.

Lenny is a superb storyteller- and excitingly engaging!

'WHO'S WHO IN THE GLADDEN FAMILY

By Ernest (aka "Doc") Gladden (1880-1939)

"Doc" Gladden, a Fayetteville/Manlius barber, has a serious heart condition and can no longer work. He whiles away the hours writing about his family. They live at 225 Mill St, Fayetteville, NY

April 2, 1938

Snow kept sifting down all day,
No spring was in the air;
And Park kept busy in the shop
A trimming up the hair.

Five and thirty years ago,
He opened up his eyes;
His Birthday, it had come again,
For him, a great surprise.

At half past nine, he closed his shop
Straight for home this night did run
Not thinking that his friends were there
To great him with some fun.

Dorothy and Roy were here (Dorothy- Marie's sister)
Mrs. Page and "sis" Marie
Pat and wife filled out the bunch

For a great surprise, you see.

Marie was hostess of the bunch,
Cocktails she served so well;
The crowd was merry- everyone
And full of merry hell.

At eleven, all were seated
Round the table, candles bright
If anyone had troubles
They were chased out for the night.

Fruit salad was so tasty,
Rolls, coffee - were ok
The cake was so delicious
And the bunch sure was gay.

The snack was over in due time
And all were gay and bright;
They all began at once to sing
And sing with all their might.

The trombone took the lead, of course,
The chorus, it was fair;
Marie played up the ivory keys.
There was music in the air

Some of the songs were very old,
And some were rather new;
The old finale came at last,
"Happy Birthday, Park, to you!

Down the road of life we ride,
A year will quickly go;
We hope we'll all together meet
And have another show.

And,as we travel down the road,

Let's do things that are worthwhile;
Let's "Scratch the other fellow's back".
And try to make him smile.

The "road of life" will end someday,
To each and every one-
Let's be kind to all our neighbors
And have a lot of fun.

"Love Thy neighbor as thyself",
It's hard, but let us try
We'll be happier for doing so
As we go passing by.

No matter what our troubles are,
Just think, they worse might be.
So, keep smiling all the while
'Til we reach Eternity.

April 3, 1938

Marie, she wore her uniform (Marie Hamilton Gladden, Crouse-Irving
Hospital- Pediatrics Charge Nurse)
To the city she did go
The air was very chilly
And we had an inch of snow.

Jennie didn't feel so hot (Jennie/Jane- Ernest's wife)
She overworked, I vow.
She drank her coffee, went to bed
And is feeling better now.

At one o'clock we had our feed,
Meat pie was nice and brown.
At five o'clock, the car rolled out.
Took Parker into town. (Parker, son of Ernest and Jane aka Jennie)

When he arrived in Syracuse,

He picked up sweet Marie.
A little hunger pain they felt
And stopped at B & B.

The snack they had so tastey,
Then a drive downtown did go,
To have some recreation
To Keith's to see a show. (RKO Keith's Movie Theater, Syracuse)

"Mad About Nurses" was the show
Diana Durbin sang,
It was a four star picture,
And went over with a bang.

Home they did come at half past ten,
A lunch, of course, they ate,
And yawning now, they went to bed
For it was getting late.

Good night, dear ones, good night.
Be happy, kind and true.
Four leaf clovers will soon grow.
We hope you'll find one, too,

April 4, 1938

Blue Monday has come again,
And nothing seems to grow.
The atmosphere is very cold,
Last night we had more snow.

Marie has gone to work again,
Park opened up his shop;
Don't feel so well myself today,
So I guess I'll take a flop.

The washer spins, and Jennie sings
The clothes are sparkling white;

Jane plans to hit the city
When Park goes tonight,

Park worked alone all day,
And business was just fair;
The snow kept falling all day long,
While he was cutting hair.

At night, he and his mother
Went in to get Marie;
And then they went to Laura's
Down old Genesee.

She just had moved into this place
"We hate it", so they say,
But soon Park stepped on the gas
For home to end the day.

I read the news and radioed,
The folks arrived at night;
We soon were snoring in our beds
To pass another night.

It's every man's duty to treat other people, a little better than they treat him.

April 6, 1938

Verse is good, the whole world knows...but, now, I'll write a little prose. At 6:50, the silence was broken! "Baby Ben"Sang out," Get up! GET UP!" But, Marie and Park just stretched and thought,"Just a few more minutes more!" And, finally they began to move at 7:05. I was up reading The Post Standard and read of the death of Lillian Bell Curtis of Manlius. The Chevy rolled into town carrying its usual morning passengers. Park soon returned and had his breakfast of "hen fruit" and toast all waiting. Jennie and Parker went into the city at 1 o'clock to pick up Marie for shopping. Jennie took two dresses to the alteration shop. Parker exchanged pants and bought some underwear. Met Rose and

Mrs. Glazier on Salina Street. Returned home at 4 bells. After dinner, Park closed the shop. He and Marie took a walk up to see Dorothy. Still cold...and this morning was the coldest of them all. With an evening drink of lemonade, we retired rather early to rest our weary bones.

April 9, 1938

Lucky seven and what a day!
The sun is bright as June.
The air is crisp, but not so cold.
We hope 't'will warm up soon.

"Scotty" wore her uniform ("Scotty"= Marie, known for her frugality)
The Chevy Park did drive.
The birds were singing in the trees,
"'Tis great to be alive!

Jane baked some tasty bread
No better could be made.
She's stepping on the gas all day,
Too much, I am afraid!

Park backed the car out on the street,
T'was early, don't you see;
And drove right down to Lincoln Hall
To hear the symphony.

Polak led the orchestra
Great music, fine, ok,
There was Alec Talbarine,
The ivories he did play.

Marie, she called the Phillips
They were happy, bright and gay
But soon Park drove up in the car
To complete another day.

So, home again on Mill Street

To spend another night,
No matter what tomorrow brings,
Just don't give up the fight

If you are perfect and say bad things about your neighbor...Jesus says,
"He that is without sin, cast the first stone."

April 10, 1938

O, weatherman! O, Weatherman!
Don't you hear the howling mob?
Give us some warm spring sunshine-
Or you may lose your job!

Marie went to the "Death House",
The medicine to give,
The undertaker needs a stiff,
They're lucky if they live!

Jennie has decided
That to Boston she will ride,
And take a short vacation
With Gen she will abide. ("Gen"= Genevieve, Park's sister)

Dorothy and Roy came down (Dorothy- Marie's sister)
The evening for to kill.
But soon they stepped upon the gas,
And went back up the hill.

Park and Marie took a ride
To Dr. Dix did go;
They soon came rolling home again,
Through all the falling snow.

Let's dream some happy dreams tonight
Let's make our lives worthwhile;
Let's scratch the other fella's back
And try to make him smile.

Be a booster, not a knocker
If you have to walk alone
If there's a real "hereafter"
You'll be sitting on the throne.

Let us bury deep the hatchet
The "pipe of peace"- let's smoke
Let's be a good Samaritan
Then life won't be a joke.

April 11, 1938

The last day of the week has come
Much snow lies on the ground;
Each night, it gets so very cold
The water sure doth freeze.

Jane has packed her bag today,
And she is full of joy;
To Syracuse, she went her way,
With Dorothy and with Roy.

Her hair all waved- she's happy
And not a bit of sorrow;
She'll be heading for Jamaican Plains
About this time tomorrow.

Park and Don slashed off the hair (Don Sutfin=Park's barbershop
partner)
The razors they were dull,
They were busy in the afternoon
At night, there was a lull.

The day was very stormy,
The wind began to blow;
The blizzard raged 'til evening
Snowplows removed the snow,

Park brought home three cans of beer
Our lips they sure did touch;
Beer is "good for what you've got":
If we don't drink too much!

Silence came near midnight
Leave that for me to tell;
Another day has passed away
And soon to sleep we fell.

Now, let us "whistle while we work";
To everyone, let's smile.
Let's help the other fellow on,
Then life will be worthwhile.

April 12, 1938

Palm Sunday has arrived again
The church bells are a ringing
We Should go to church today
And help out with the singing.

The Gladdens, they are sleeping,
Whils't our neighbors trudge through snow,
And the sermon that they will get
Will be on the radio.

At 8:15, I went downstairs
And coffee, I did make
An egg and toast will satisfy
For good old stomach's sake.

Jane arises; Parker next
And have a bite to eat.
But soon they're off to Syracuse
The Central train to meet.

Good bye! So long, to Jennie
Much joy and needed rest;
We'll keep the fires a-burning
We'll do our level best.

Marie worked in the kitchen
The grub, she did prepare.
Dot and Roy came down at two
And Parker cut my hair.

The table soon was spread with food,
And all were filled with joy,
Who ate the most, we could not tell
Was it Park, or was it Roy?

I think 'twas Roy who won the race,
As judge, I must allow,
He works all night and early morn
Upon the old snow plough.

April 14, 1938

"Old Sol" and I arose at about the same time. It seemed like a different world. And did HE, reinforced by the balmy breezes of "Dixie" snow, completely put the snow to route. The robin comes out of hiding and sings for us again. The blades of grass woke up again and raised their wee hands to the heavens. It was great to be alive again and look upon our beautiful world! Our lives are made up of clouds and sunshine. Yes- clouds of sorrow or the sunshine of happiness. As some poet hath said:"What is the use of repining? Where there's a will, there's a way." Tomorrow the sun may be shining- although it's cloudy today. Marie has gone to the hospital and Tony ("aka Parker") to the butcher shop. No doubt that before the day is ended, a patient may be sent to the Crouse Irving for repairs. I am the "chief cook and bottle washer", doing a swell job and loving it! No one has needed a doctor today...yet. Marie came home early and prepared the dinner. I can taste the haddock yet. Ate too much and paid for it later! Guess Jane and her mother are dining

out this evening. Have a good time, Jane- but don't let your waistline
get too long!!

April 15, 1938

Marie went on her job again
And Park picked up his shears;
Just the same old daily routine
They've been following now for years.

Marie knocked off early
In the kitchen she did "toil",
After dinner was all over
Half a ham she put to boil.

So, you see, we never go hungry-
All the Gladdens love to feed
Marie digs her garden up
Soon, it's ploughing for the seed.

The day has ended beautifully,
The moon is shining bright
If we've been good to all we've met
Then I will say Goodnight!

April 16, 1938

There's sunshine on the earth this morn
The grass is growing fast;
We'd like to live a few days more
For Spring is here at last!

At one, Park went to Syracuse,
And nothing could be nicer
He went to bring home sweet Marie
And little Connie Spicer. (Marie's young patient)

Connie talks a mile a minute

And romps from noon to night
She's different from the Gladdens
She has no appetite.

She's just as sweet as sweet could be
Has azure eyes of blue,
She's four years old and tiny-
Only weighs thirty-two.

Phillips came out later
She had dinner with us all;
She's a nurse and always smiling
A dark-haired girl and rather small.

A holy, holy day it was!
And ham she could not take
Fish just melted in her mouth
Not from Oneida lake!

Genevieve and Jennie
Are happy as can be
They'll celebrate Gen's birthday
For she is thirty-three.

Now, Gen, you've reached the half-way mark
Upon the road of life;
We hope the sun shines always
Never having any strife.

April 18, 1938

For the next few days, we'll do our writing in prose. Have been too busy
to write much since Jane went to Jamaica Plains. Park and Marie took
their usual ride to Crouse-Irving Hospital. Everybody is sprucing up
for Easter and "Tony" (Park) is very busy. Don is playing rummy for
his daily bread and takes whiskey for a chaser. Park is sore at him and
the storm may break very soon. I laundered some clothes and reclined
much. Didn't feel so good. Marie came home early and prepared our

evening meal. I radioed much in the evening and Park and Marie went for a ride. Here's hoping for a more better day.

April 19, 1938

It's cold and runny today. In the morning Post Standard is a picture of Mike Havel and his big trout he caught in Limestone Creek. The whistling mailman brought a letter from Gen.This isn't Black Friday - but Good Friday- the anniversary of the Burial of Christ. Let is all bury our hatred, our jealousies, and envy this day and fill our hearts with more love for our neighbors. Don't censor the other fella-Perhaps if you were in his place, you would do no better than he.

April 19, 1938

The sun came up smiling and Mother Nature was all around. The Northern Lights or Aurora Borealis flashed through the heavens last night. Don is rather "sick" today (again) and is of little help. At closing time, he got the warning and a vacation til the end of next week. Better straighten up- Don-or you'll be scouting for another job.After work, Park and Marie went in to see Dr. Dix and returned at midnight. Do ye unto others as you would have done unto you. Don't misinterpret and "Do unto others before they do it unto you."

April 20, 1938

The joyous Easter Day is here,
The day is fair and bright,
The pious are a parading
To church from morn till night.

"Love THY neighbor as thyself"
Jesus Christ hath said-
So -let us do this everyday
Or- be a long time dead.

Never have too much to say,
Think twice before you speak

Be good-natured all the day
Be loving, and be kind.

April 22, 1938

Our national game of baseball opens today.And I listened in on the A's
and the Senators.Washington won-3 to 1 and FDR threw out the first
ball.A beautiful morning but it rained in the afternoon. Roy was here
and announced that his boss was giving him a "vacation." (aka being
fired!). Park as very busy and didn't get home for supper; Marie carried
it to him. Don't always tell the truth. If a little lie brings happiness
instead of tears-tell the lie.Never say anything that may hurt the other
fella's feelings.

April 24, 1938

Marie has planted her sweet peas. Soon they will be a peeping through.
Let us plant seeds of love and kindness in our gardens of character,
"Would ye sow what ye also shall reap?" Water that garden with smiles
and let the sunshine of happiness shine upon it. All the world will love
such a garden! I didn't feel so good today but why tell you my troubles?
You have plenty of your own. Park went to Lincoln Hall today to hear
the symphony. He LOVES his music. But, as we love music, children
and pets know no detective will be on our trail. Forget the past..that's
where it is- in the past! And why worry about the morrow?

April 25, 1938

Westward goes the Chevy
Marie bailed out on Crouse
Park stepped on the gas again
And came back to the house.

Half day for "Scotty"- home again
Stepping like a winner,
Jane and Charles were coming soon (Charles- Marie's brother)
To eat a six layer dinner.

Seven bells and Charles drove in
Rose was invited, too
We sat down at the table
No one was feeling blue.

Charles loves a six-layer dinner
And ate and ate and ate.
But soon they drove on westward
For it was getting late.

The Chevvy rolled out later
The gas and air to mix-
They glided into Syracuse
To visit Dr. Dix.

April 26, 1938

The clouds silently slipped away and the sun is smiling down on the green fields today. The "Maple Leafs" were scattered to the tune of 3 to 1. Park had worked the whole week long...alone. He took some time off in the afternoon and picked some dandylion greens. They make a good poultice for the stomach or what have you. Don has been "thinking" all week (conditional firing)- is sober on the job today! Hope he learns that a business and drinking do not mix! It's the old story- "A fool and his money are soon parted!"

April 27, 1938

A two and a seven make up this date
A day with clouds overhead,
Not every day the shine will shine-
So the poet said!

The Municipal Park was wet-
No ball game they did play.
But the "Ball Game of Life"
Must be played each and every day!

"Time" is pitching to all of us
And the crowd begins to shout
Keep your eye on the horse-hide
Never let them strike you out!

Two strikes - three balls is the count
Just one more time must throw.
There it comes right o'er the middle
You MUST swing or down you go!

You swing with all your might-
The ball - you hit it true
It sails out o'er the middle wall
A HOME RUN goes for you!

Park and Don are very busy
The clippers trimmed their hair
The first part of the week was dull
But now- it's rather fair!

Marie comes home at five o'clock
Park worked til half past eight
They stayed at home this evening
A tasty snack they ate.

Have we been nice to everyone-
That we have met today?
Have we been a listener-
Not had too much to say?

Be merry with the merry
And sympathize with the woe-
We'll always have a wealth of friends
As through life we must go.

April 28, 1938

A little frost upon the roof

Was the first to meet my eye-
The birds were singing just the same
No cloud was in the sky.

The Easy Washer turned on again
Jane used the Ivory soap
Park's business was very dull
Marie dished out her dope.

Machines are cutting down the lawns
Their noise, we like to hear
Warmer days have come again,
Now we can love our beer!

The Chiefs played Montreal today
The fans had loads of fun.
The Chiefs had their catting eye
And beat them - two to one.

Park brought home a leg of lamb
He surely likes his meat:
But, we all get in life each day
Is what we wear and eat.

Eat, drink and be merry
Be gay from foot to head-
We're living in the present
Too soon- we may be dead.

I listened to the baseball game broadcast. The "Red Birds" sure pulled all the feathers out of the Chiefs' hats! Bet them a double-header 7-4 and 8-1. Like countless number of fans,I was disgusted. But the home team is compared to our everyday lives. If we are prosperous enough and win the game of life everyday, everybody cheers and we have a host of would-be friends! But, let adversity and trouble come- and they begin to knock and find fault! "Laugh- and the world DOES laugh with you... Weep and you will weep alone."

April 29, 1938

This is the Sabbath Day
And just to make this rhyme-
If you miss your rest at night
You'll need to sleep- sometime!

Park and Marie arose at ten
And in the Chevvy rode.
They went to get some good, dark earth
And brought home quite a load.

Marie sure loves her garden
The soil must be just right-
Some of the seeds are planted
And the margin painted white.

Alone we had our dinner
Park cleaned his barber shop-
And soon the Chevvy rolled North-
Near Phoenix it did stop.

Park made the clippers hum today,
Don came in at half past ten
They cut the hair from ladies fair
And whiskers from the men.

Jane does not feel so hot
Her troubles she must face-
She'll take the train on Sunday
To see her sister, Grace.

I listened to the ball game
Mayor Marvin bought a seat,
The Bisons played the better ball,
The Chiefs went to defeat.

Down the street of "By and By", one arrives at the house of "Never".
Procrastination is the thief of time.

The weather sure is beautiful,
The sun shines every day -
No clouds mar up the sky at night
You can see the milky way!

The leaves are halfway on the trees
The grass is growing fast
It makes us happy once again
For Spring has come at last.

Park is very grouchy
His business is not fair
He closed the place at eight o'clock
And walked out in the air.

He drove into the city
Marie was in the spot-
He drove her up to Dr. Dix
And there she got her shot.

There's a Reaper whose name is Death,
And with his sickle keen
He reaps the bearded grain at a breath
And all flowers that grow between.

May 2, 1938

The weather is fine-we need a rain
Ol' Sol is smiling through:
The grass needs cutting on our lawn
And dandy-lions, too.

The Chiefs and Bisons played a game-
Balls and strikes did mix;
The Bisons won so easily,

The score was three to six.

The sun was down and Elaine came
The stars were shining bright,
She's talking very sternly
Of quitting Mrs. White.

Schramm wants to sell his restaurant
Business- rather slow
Mrs. Bull would like to buy
And make a pile of dough

May 3, 1938

It was eighty-six today
Too hot for any use
But Parker took his mother
Down to Syracuse.

Jennie had some dresses fixed
Marie- she bought a coat
Park taxied them from place to place-
These women get my goat!

Home they came at four o'clock
With spirits rather low
Park oiled up the mower,
And the lawn, he began to mow.

Let us mow the "Lawn of Life"-
the weeds of hate destroy.
The "seeds of envy"- never sow.
Plant out "the tree of joy"!

May 4, 1938

The apple trees are full of bloom,
The cherry blossoms fall-

The pie plant spreads its spaciousness-
Green onions begin to grow.

Down the street of "By and By" one arrives at the house called: "Never".
Procrastination is the thief of time.

May 5, 1938

At six-fifteen, Park arose
And walked a mile or so;
The morn was cool and cloudy
Almost cold enough to snow.

Jane took the bus to Syracuse
No rain was in the air;
To "Arch and Ellas" Shoppe
To have them set her hair.

A black handbag she bought
Two bucks paid for the purse.
It was Gen's birthday present
Jane thought it was nice.

With business bad and weather cool,
Time passed just the same;
I would have liked it better
Had there been a baseball game.

The day passed by and shadows fell
It was quiet and oh, so calm
Elsie and her sister came
To have a talk with Schramm.

Elsie hopes to buy the place
Gin, wine and ale she'll sell-
Some Irish stew and frogs legs, too
How much? No one can tell.

She'll make a cheerful hostess
Your wants she'll take to heart
She graduated from the school
Of culinary art.

Where do you think you are going when you "shuffle off? It won't be
on "the streets of gold" unless you have more consideration for the
underdog. It won't put "mud" on your clothes to say, "Good Morning!"
to the guy in the "gutter". It might help him to get out when he realizes
that someone still thinks he's a human being! Give him a hand and be
happy!

May 5, 1938

Four and fifty years ago
The stork flew over town.
He sailed o'er Freddie Parker's (Sampson Parker, Cazenovia)
And dropped a baby down.

Fred didn't want a baby girl
His language was profane
Mary loved the little mite
And so they called her Jane.

Years passed by and she was shy
And she was quite a gal!
She played with other girls in town
But Edith was her pal.

When she was seventeen years old
The boys came in her life
Gladden was more serious-
Asked her to be his wife!

One night I called to see her
She lived upon the hill-
I popped the question... "Marry me?"
Her answer- "Yes- Of course, I will!"

On June 16th, at twelve o'clock
The Wedding March we heard
The rice was scattered o'er us
We were as happy as the birds.

She eighteen, I twenty-two
Still "wet behind the ears"
We never thought of troubles
That come along in years.

I ran a shop in Congo (nickname for Corning, NY)
Then Athens was our home
We wanted not for anything
But loved to roam and roam.

A college town, we loved it
And there one early morn
When the apple blossoms opened-
Geneiveve was born.

Three years we lived in Athens
It seemed to be like Heaven.
One day we came to Manlius
In nineteen hundred seven

It seemed that everywhere we went
Four-leaf clovers grew;
Life was sweet and lovely
Disappointments very few.

In nineteen hundred twenty-nine
It surely was our fate
The dollars for our "rainy day"
We lost in real estate.

Jennie's been a good old pal
Took the bitter with the sweet.

Just meet this Jennie Gladden
And my story is complete.

May 7, 1938

Sunday and the first of May
Marie was working all the day.
Jennie took the train, you see-
Newark was her destiny.

We drove with caution in the hills
Marie was handing out her pills.
We came back to Salina Street,
Walked in a place- began to eat.

The food was grand; we cleaned the plate
The service was fine- we didn't wait.
To Fayetteville we rolled and there
Park soon was trimming up the hair.

Upon a bed, I took a flop
While Park was cleaning up the shop
The evening came; I stayed home
Park and Marie began to roam
Down at Keith's- they saw a show
They liked it much, then home did go.

May 2

The day was gloomy and cool. Business went on as usual. Marie went
to the city to "bargain with the "Undertaker". Park began scraping
faces and trimming wigs. No baseball game, so that it was rather dull
for me. Thought of Jane occasionally down in Union, NJ. Hope she
is feeling fine. In the evening, Parker and Falso went to the opera.Net
proceeds of the same went to the Mission Charity funds. Marie went
up To Dorothy's in the evening.

May 3

Toast and coffee we did eat,
Before Park started up the street
To cut the hair and shave the chins
That's just the way the day begins.

He's busy and we're so glad!
Came home for lunch and hamburg had.
The "whistling mailman" came at ten
He had a letter from our Gen.

We find that they are full of joy,
We wish they'd have a baby boy.

Park didn't come home at five fifteen
Haircuts were coming fast.
The clippers were a humming
But he finished up at last.

Marie went to a party
She was the honored nurse
If she and Park don't get more rest,
They'll be riding in the hearse.

May 4

The sky is clear; the air is cool
The Chevvy rolled along.
The birds were singing in the trees
Their early morning songs.

We had some scrambled eggs for lunch,
Some bacon on the side
Some hash browns, fried potatoes
Which really satisfied.

In the afternoon, Marie came home
She cooked a six-layer dinner

No better meal could e'er be served
To saint or to a sinner.

"Phillips" came to this repast
And so did Dot and Roy
It disappeared like magic
We ate with so much joy.

May 5

I did not feel so well today-
Yet, why should I complain?
We can not have all sunshine
Some days, it's bound to rain.

Park brought home veal cutlet,
I fried it nice and brown
And with the dishes on the side
A feed of great reknown.

The Chiefs were beaten - 5 to 3
Baseball they cannot play
They'd better wake up at once
Or, in the cellar they'll stay.

Meatballs and spaghetti
At five o'clock, we ate
We took a ride to Orville
When it was getting late.

The new drugstore was open
We had a soda all around
Then Parker stepped upon the gas
And we were homeward bound.

The lightning flashed, the thunder roared
We need all the rain
The farmers were delighted.

For it will cure their grain.

May 9

The furnace fire I kindled
The air was full of chill
The Chevvy rolled on smoothly
To Crouse Irving on the hill.

Toast and eggs we ate for breakfast
Park stalked up and down there,
With all his skill and science
Began to cut the hair.

Some farmer from the hills came in
You could scarcely see an ear
He hadn't had a haircut
For nigh unto a year!

Park started up the clippers
The shears began to squeeze-
When he was finished cutting off his locks
Hair was piled to his knees.

May 10

As a rule, man's a fool
When it's hot, he wants cold;
When it's cool, he wants it hot-
Always wanting what is not!

Today, it's cool with clouds o'er head
If the sun don't shine- we'll all be dead.
But let us smile and smile
The sun may shine in a little while.

Bahouth is spading up the dirt,
Go easy, George, your back may hurt,

Peas and beans he'll plant today,
His garden sure will pay and pay.

The soil is rich and mellow, too
'Twill grow most anything for you.
Alone, Park to the city went
And for supplies some change he spent.

He used to spend some for booze
Today he bought a pair of shoes.
Heard Marie come home at three
The washing she will do, you see.

Two letters came today from Jane
She's coming home soon on the train
She is not feeling well
And really worse than she will tell.

I tuned in the radio
'Tis grand - this Tuesday show!

May 11

Old Sol! Old Sol! Where have you gone?
Your face you hide away.
Can't you push those clouds away
And bring a sunny day?

Marie has done all the washing
Most of the ironing -too,
I cook and wash the dishes
That's all that I can do.

Marie went down to see Dr. Dix
And for her protection
Gave her a shot and opened up
A finger with infection.

Parker was not too busy
And business rather slow-
He bought two razors from a guy
For fifty cents or so.

May 12

Cool breezes blowing all day long
The rain is falling fast
We hope for better days to come
That this will be our last.

Park hustled to the barber shop
Marie went on the hill,
I kept the home fires burning
The oil stove I did fill.

At five p.m.Park drove away
To meet the choo-choo train
His mother came from Union
All the time it poured down rain,

At six o'clock they pulled in home
And Jane was not so well
Park went out in the evening
To the Syracuse Hotel.

The nurses had a party there
They danced round and round
Near midnight, "Home, Sweet Home" they played
Then they were homeward bound.

May 13

This gloomy day is Friday
And the number is thirteen
Be careful what you do today
It's NOT lucky- that I mean.

The white flame of the oil stove
Keeps warming up the house
Jane finished up the laundry
As quiet as a mouse,

The Bisons and the Chiefs play ball
Buffalo wins the game.
A home run with the bases full
The score was not the same.

Marie came home at 6 p.m.
Park closed up at nine,
I listened to "Death Valley Days"
Was feeling very fine.

The moon shone bright all evening
A way up in the sky,
A full eclipse was scheduled
For this moon by and by.

The eclipse began at half past one
When the heavens were so bright
At half past three, the moon was dark
And we received no light.

May 14

The south wind blows today
The moon is bright and fair.
This is a busy time for Park
A clipping off the hair.

The Chiefs play the Bisons
Up at Buffalo
The Bisons nearly won the game
They started off too slow.

Marie came home early
She usually comes at eight-
Park was very busy
And didn't close til late.

We sat out in the kitchen
Park bought a pint of rum
Cocktails were made to order
No one was feeling bum.

No one went out this evening
At "Home, Sweet Home" we stayed.
We listened to the radio
Then in our bunks we laid.

May 15

Marie has to work today
Left home a little late
Park stepped upon the gas
Was home soon after eight.

Jane is feeling better
At eight was on her feet
Her appetite is picking up
Toast and egg she sure did eat.

Park went up to the barber shop
And tidied up the place
Jane was cooking dinner
I was shaving up my face.

It rained and rained, the cold wind blew
A fire we had all day
We surely needed more sunshine
In this "merry" month of May.

Marie and Park went down to Keiths

To see the evening show
Jane crossed the street to see the Sheams
I tuned the radio.

May 16

This is not a blue Monday
The clouds have passed away
The sun is shining once again
It's beautiful today!

It's just another day though
The wash is on the line
Park is scraping chins again
And business is going fine.

The Maple Leafs played the Chiefs
And they had alot of fun
The Chiefs were mighty at the bat
The score was eight to one.

The Hatches are our neighbors
Fred Hatch, a plumber is;
They're good, old-fashion people
And they always mind their biz.

When twilight falls, they go to bed
Their house they sure adore
When morning comes, they're feeling fine
Now- who could ask for more?

May 17

This morning we had pancakes
And they were steaming hot
The java was a perking
In that same old coffee pot.

Jane is slowly convalescing
Can step around once more
She irons, dusts and sweeps
And washes up the floor.

We had swiss steak for dinner
Good enough for any king
Mary came in at six o'clock
And overalls did bring.

Picnic time will soon be here
Overalls the girls will wear
That good old Sunday picnic
Will beat a county fair.

Mary works in the garden
The flowers she loves to grow
She pulverizes the ground
And plants them in a row.

May 18

Marie has gone to Syracuse
To wait upon the sick,
Once more Jane hops about the house
With steps so sure and quick.

Toronto beat the Chiefs today
Six runs Toronto made
Syracuse got none at all
A goose-egg sure was laid.

Marie came home at five o'clock
The supper cooked for Park
They worked out in the garden
Till it was almost dark.

May 19

Don is on the job today
To help out hustling "Tony" (Park aka "Tony")
Jane prepared our noon day lunch
Of cheese and macaroni.

Marie's infected finger
Has healed up mighty fast
The balmy air is blooming
Warm days have come at last.

In front, the shrubbery bloom again
In the rear, the garden grows
We'll all enjoy the summer months
From now til wintry snows.

May 20

This has been National Air Mail week. Much celebration all over the country. A plane carried mail from our village. The high school band was out and most of the students. Mr. White has moved his drug store to the Costello block, corner of N. Mill and E. Genesee. The Chiefs scalped the Newark Bears- 6 to 5 in a 13 inning game. LUCKY THIRTEEN! Marie came home early. She and Park took a ride in the evening. Jane is feeling much better again.

May 21

Marie goes to the hospital. Beautiful day and not too hot! A new fad-I see two women mowing their lawns! Gosh darn it! Men won't have a thing to do soon! Did you say our Chiefs could play ball? They beat Newark Niners- 4 to 3! Park and Marie drove to Bersani's for refreshment. I blew the foam off a glass of beer myself before they departed.

May 22

What a beautiful day! I dressed and went out in the sunshine. OH! How Beautiful! Hung around the premises for most of the morning.

Along came Fred Goodfellow. First time I had seen Fred in 16 months. Went uptown with Park - first time since August 1937. We took a drive to Onondaga Hill. Back in an hour and had roast duck for dindin. I listened to the Chiefs and Orioles playing ball in Baltimore. Will be getting out every day now. Hope to be working again soon, too. Sure have the desire- and hopefully the strength.

May 23

Park and his mate rolled westward
Their daily bread to earn,
The boss stopped at the barber shop
And made the fire to burn.

The day was nice, I dressed at 2
And walked uptown once more
To meet my old acquaintances
And see White's new store

On the corner of N. Mill Street
And the busy Genesee
The best location in town
Good business there will be.

I wandered in the store nearby
John Burt I wished to see
"Skipper" still is working there
For the good ol' company.

The same old place is Willits
The loafers there would meet
All kinds of chance devices
Your fortune there to seek.

Then I went up to the barber shop
'Twas looking mighty fine
Next place was old man Kanter
Selling California wine.

It was a glorious morning
Many people I did meet
11:30 found me home
Two twenty five Mill Street.

GRAVE SECRETS

"Grave Secrets" is a Reader's Theatre presentation of personalities from the grave. These unique individuals intentionally "sound off" often humorously, insightfully, bitterly and always honestly grave. Running Time" 60 minutes.

The play was premiered at The RivolI Theatre, S. Fallsburg, May 10,11,12, 2013 by The Sullivan County Dramatic

Workshop Written/. Directed by Sally Gladden

Cast: Ed Berens, Stephanie Watson, Wayne Kuetcher, Alicia Kahn, Leroy Wright, Adam Dohrenwend, Sally Gladden. Theatre Association of NY Excellence Award.

GRAVE SECRETS, a READERS' THEATRE PRESENTATION by Sally Gladden

BLACK OUT. Music: "I Can See Clearly Now" from movie: "Cool Runnings" during which time lights slowly come up to view grave stones and 3 people sitting/posed on both platforms. These six portray several characters.

The scene is NOT eerie, scary or ghastly but rather a pleasant day in the cemetery. NOTE: script entries denoted by [ ] probably/possibly cutting.

ENTER NARRATOR. MUSIC fades out a Narrator takes the stand. (gestures to the tombstones.) a la "Under Milkwood" style

NARRATOR: (Edit at will) People are dying to get in there! Please know that this scene is not one from "The Walking Dead" or "The Zombies Walk Among Us"! No! No— "Grave Secret's or Secrets From the Grave takes place in a pleasant cemetery on a pleasant day. I will admit that I have been influenced by Edgar Lee Master's "Spoon River

Anthology" and Wilder's, "Our Town". I decided that I would write my own messages from deceased people.

[Omit??] When I was a child, Dad would take me to visit his parents. Often mom and dad would journey over to visit with mom's parents in Syracuse. They were all deceased! Dad's mom and dad resided n the Manlius, NY Cemetery. Mostly middle-class folks here. There was a huge fountain where we would dip our buckets. Usually this was a coffee tin and then we would water the flowers. Lilacs were the flower of choice. Lilacs are for remembrance! While dad chatted with his parents, Jane and Ernest Gladden, I would investigate all the other grave sites.

Mom's mother, father and step mother were all resting in Woodlawn Cemetery located near Syracuse University, a cemetery of quite affluent residents. Here there were acres of monuments and mausoleums to explore. One of the most terrific sites for me was visiting a huge granite mausoleum. Mausoleums fascinated me. A large one was up on a hill. On Sundays, guests could walk through the quiet place that had a few tufts of flowers here and there on some of the residents' shelves. Throughout the years, these all became plastic flowers. Undoubtedly the surviving loved ones did not have to visit the place that often. Easy maintenance. No watering needed here. It was such fun to take favorite friend to this place to walk through the echoy halls of this huge mausoleum. The slightest footsteps could be heard in that huge empty space. Most of my friends were thrillingly scared because of the coldness, and the dampness and the eerie sounds you would hear. Myself—I just liked the cold feeling there. I never could understand why people would prefer to be stacked up in these walls upon others. The interior of this place could accommodate these 5 or 6 tiers of people who rested there. My dad said that some people were very afraid of having dirt shoveled over them and they chose to be interred in a mausoleum thus avoiding a grave. But, I digress.

Our frequent visits to these cemeteries were an exciting part of MY education. I was never bored. I usually found other activities to do such as scampering from monument to headstone, or trying to figure out the age of the deceased. I learned to subtract!. DOB and DOD became a worthwhile numbers exercise for me. I tried to envision the person who resided there just by the carving on the monument albeit most headstones were designed AFTER their person died. [omit?? Some

monuments were extravagant. Other stones were for small children...
and babies.

Some of these were the most precious and the parents paid mightily
for a little lamb, or a small child perpetually holding up her hand to the
heavens. Some areas were more opulent. One could pay for a "resting
bench", "a tree" or a mighty statue that would be taller than another
one. Most cemeteries have walls surrounding their inhabitants.

Some family plots had cast iron fences around their plots. Funny—
are the fences there to keep people in... or keep them out? Tombstone
carvings are either very ornate or plain. Some survivors had money
enough to pay for engravings and epitaphs such as "Loved Forever" or
"Beloved wife and mother". We know how affluent these resting people
were by the quality, size and elaborate stones each has. My parents were
the only survivors of their families and hadn't much money ;the grave
stones are rather plain. Mom's father must have paid for his because that
plot's heasdtone is rather ornate.

So—allow me to share with you some voices from their graves.

1—My name is Helen Evans. I stay to myself here. I bother no one and
no one bothers me. I taught Latin for 25 years before I was urged
by the principal to retire. My classroom was run strictly. Young men
and young ladies had to stand in front of the class and conjugate and
decline. If there was any mistake, he or she would have to start over.

Discipline! That's what young people needed. They certainly
need more discipline today! The idea—that a parent would dare
confront me about MY teaching methods. It is true that some of
these children broke down in tears. I recall that Denise ran out
of the room crying. **I** did not humiliate her—she brought it on
herself by not knowing her lesson! She was failing anyway. There
is no room for any mistakes. We need to DEMAND excellence...
not mediocrity! The principal called me into his office to talk
about the incident... and my teaching methods. "Wasn't I being
too hard on the kids?" "Wasn't I concerned about THEIR self-
esteem?" Foolishness. That's how I was taught. I learned Not to
make mistakes! A good student entering college would HAVE to
know Latin, wouldn't he? Latin was removed from the curriculum.
I was removed from my classroom. Instead young teachers were
brought in to teach Spanish and French. What do they know of

teaching? They played games and sang songs! Foolishness! Their noise was exceedingly disruptive to My classes. Since I was an experienced, TENURED teacher, (THEY COULDN'T FIRE ME!) They found other duties for me. I became a resource teacher... my task was to help slow... usually struggling students with their papers. Then I was Vice-Principal which didn't last too long. They just shuffled me anywhere.

Finally I was given incentive to retire early. (Bitterly) And I took it! Anyway the entire school was being over-run by "wetbacks" and others of their type. I got even. I had rarely taken any sick days in all the years I taught so I had a plan. My last year, I called in sick every day and they always had to get a substitute. I showed Them!

2—John. John Tucci... age 18. I don't know how it happened. to ME! ME! Me and addict! I was everyone's friend. I had just started taking some classes at the local community college. I met new people. A few parties later I was was really into marijuana... lots. God, I was popular! Girls hung all over me. Heck—no one ever died from a little pot. Somehow I needed more... different drugs to get me thru. Met more friends at these parties... and different drugs. Some guy from the city brought in heavier drugs... easy for them to get. My girl—Fran—would keep on nagging me to "slow down"... you gotta get some help. I worry about you." Naw – I kept telling her I was ok... I knew when to stop. Everybody knew they could come to me for good stuff. I was connected. I had friends. Don't know how it got out of control... I really needed to get high! I knew when to stop... Parents divorced... classes got harder... more demanding... I helped myself to "feeling good stuff"... We all lied to our parents about staying over at a friends'... the guys from the city brought in some excellent stuff. Snorted cocaine—for the first time! God what a rush! Soon I liked it. I felt great! In December, right around Christmas time—a few of got together. Just a simple holiday party! A kid brought heroin. Heck—nothing happened to me when I snorted coke—what the hell... He said it was pure stuff and I needed to go easy. All I remember is feeling... no flying... Then nothing. They all shouted "What's the matter with him? Help him!" They picked me up and carried me out to the park, put me on a bench

and split. They just left me there! Cause of death—drug overdose.
It wasn't supposed to get this far...

3—My epitaph! As a BUSY housewife I FINALLY got to sleep in!!!
Me? I'm nobody special. I am... I am just a housewife. Funny that
word... like I was married to the house. I always wanted to be the
best mom I could be. My mom didn't work... oh— you know—she
didn't have an outside job... outside of doing all the house chores.
I wanted to be like her—be there when the kids came home for
school, helping with the PTO, being a den mother for the scouts,
being here when my husband needed me. I lived for many years
as a contented housewife. Women's Libbers would get on my case.
They'd suggest that I care more about ME. Go to the gym, have an
affair, drink, or join a book club... things like that. I did NONE of
those things... nor did I watch day-time soaps. With 4 kids, 2 cats
and our dog—I was ALWAYS busy. And then there was Jim—a
devoted father and husband. It was IMPORTANT that he would
come home to a happy home... not just a house. Our home was
spotless... Our children were respectful. Meals were always on the
table at the right time... dependable time. Why—every Wednesday
was our night for... making love. I don't believe I was ever bored
or discontent. I was just ALWAYS busy. Well—maybe too busy to
take care of my own health. Everyone else came first and I tried
not to be a bother to anyone. I learned to be a martyr—mother...
from MY mother. The day I died? Well—I was carrying a load of
laundry downstairs and—somehow I tripped. I fell. I recall lying at
the foot of the stairs... I couldn't move. The dog was looking at me.
He nuzzled me to get up. I could not move anything.
     I was paralyzed. At the hospital they told my family that had
severe brain damage. I was in an "'irreversible coma". After a week,
my husband signed the papers to have me taken off life supports.
We had Never talked about death—or what would happen IF, or,
when... we were just going to have the kids grow up, leave and start
their own families. And we would grow old together... just Jim
and me... til "death do us part". I had no fancy dress to be buried
in so Jim chose a skirt and sweater. I was always GOING to get
myself a gorgeous dress for some special occasion... to feel pretty
again. Someday! I said SOMEDAY... alot. How sad that people live

their lives around SOMEDAYS... someday I'm going to go here, someday I'm going to speak up... someday. Well—you know—we NEVER get another chance to live our one life. I would not build my life around somedays... I would act on these wishes... these dreams... hopes... plans. I would not defer them to a SOMEDAY.... Jim remarried 6 months after my funeral. Oh. My name is Nancy Wright Britten.

4—Frank Griffith. Aged 90. What a wonderful life! Not like some of these poor folks who are sleeping here. I died of OLD AGE and I died peacefully. Folks were farmers... poor farmers. Had to quit school at age 14 to help with the farm. The Great Depression in the early 30's wiped out many families and what little possessions they had. I entered the Civilian Job Corps. So many young people from all over the country were learning trades. I was sent to Arizona. The little I was paid I sent home to mom and pop. Raising 6 children was tough for them. Everyone had to pitch in and help out. We were a close knit, God fearing family. And I thank God for being in my life ALWAYS. Married a gal in 1940—my only sweetheart... Margie. At that time, Uncle Sam was calling HARD and LOUD... and I wanted to help my country. Signed on to the Navy. I sure grew up a lot in the 3 years of active duty. Will never forget Pearl Harbor. But I don't want to talk about it. Lost too many buddies... it hurts alot. God! Country! and family were what mattered to me... to us. I won't complain about any of the hardships... we stuck together as a family. In those days-neighbors helped neighbors. Always thought on my death bed when asked if I had made peace with God... I always wanted to say—just like Thoreau said when he was ready to go... "I wasn't aware that we had quarreled!!" Lived a life I would do all again! Well—my final words were: "Guess I'm about done, Lord!" My wife is next to me here. 2 still-born children are here. My daughter brings her brew by sometimes... but the visits are lesser and lesser. They are busy! Everyone is busy... busy... busy!

5—Damn it! I told them I was sick! Name's Fred Drake. Age upon death 57. Finally my nagging cough seems to be a bit better! Doctors called it emphysema—fancy name for coughing my lungs out! My lungs were shot. At least the coughing and the smoking doesn't bother "HER" anymore! The wife would constantly bitch, "So do something about that awful cough, Fred!" Was a cigarette smoker for decades—smoked as a kid; smoked in the Army. Proud veteran of WW 2!—smoked all through work at the paper mill where I worked—fags didn't kill me—I swear that her nagging did!

Constant nagging. But—heck—she was a good old girl, my Martha. Got no complaints about my life 'cept I ain't living no more! But these damned kids around here—tipping over gravestones for kicks. Monuments lovingly put up by families of the deceased... they think it's fun to smash 'em. I'd like to smash a few of these rotten kids! Drinking—partying here in this cemetery. We get no respect around here. No respect! Cripe, when I was young my buddies and I would have fun—get drunk in the woods, tip over a cow or an outhouse—but we'd NEVER think of disrespecting the folks in cemeteries. This be where we are resting our last rest! These rotten kids today got too much time on their hands don't know the meaning of the four letter word WORK. Those kids will get theirs someday—and I don't mean just the law—the BIG LAW—when we all become equal in death! This is OUR resting place and—well—the other night the Ghost Tour people came trapsing through the cemetery... 14 of them—wanting to see ghosts. You'd think folks would have something better to do than look for ghosts. Ain't gunna tell you we are or are not. (Wink) I'd like to have given them a ghost (Gesture!) This is OUR resting place—here everyone is finally equal. Don't have nothing more to say.

6—I am Delroy Wright... I spent my childhood in Albany, Georgia. Born 1944. Maybe you never heard of the place.

Guess the only famous person from there was Ray Charles. But he wasn't too proud of being from Albany where Blacks were second class citizens. Jim Crow laws remained Down South for too many years. Life changed when Reverend Martin Luther King came to our church. Gave a beautiful, rousing sermon and started us thinking that WE were Americans too. We were to go peacefully after our rights just as Jesus would have done! Just as Ghandi would have done! The journey wasn't going to be easy. I was just 16 and some organizer folks from New York... Freedom Riders they called themselves... met with us. We were all to go to the Woolworth's Store in downtown Albany and sit... just sit at the counter... and when they come to take us away we were to offer no resistance. After all—we were just sitting there—doing no harm. We really wanted to just enjoy a coke with vanilla ice cream float. Odd, huh—one of the finest sodas was a dark coke (like me) with a blob of white ice crème (like you)... mixing together to make a fine soda! We was just wanting to sit and relax just like other folks at Woolworth's that day! Yes—we were arrested for breaking their law! Then we were called – Negroes... and a bunch of other names that's for sure! Today we are Blacks... or African-Americans. We learned that we are ALL equal in the sight of God—doesn't matter whose God... especially in America! We could never understand why some people were more equal than others... back then! We had the money to buy the sodas but it was against THEIR laws back then... A spunky woman—named Rosa Parks had just made news... that she refused to give up her seat on the bus to a white man—cuz she was just plain tired! I moved up north here—raised a family—all 6 of my children are in good professions—lawyering, teaching and the like. Ya know—after growing up in the segregated South—there are finally NO signs there that read "FOR COLOREDS ONLY".

7—I always wanted to go first. Name's Lawrence McDoogle. Married 51 years to the love of my life... my only sweet gal. I started to fall down—alot—and my hearing started to go. I tried my best to look out for my Mary. Each day she became worse—there were days she didn't know me at all. They called it Alzheimer's... dementia. Daughter thought we both should go into a nursing home where they could care for us daily. Daughter put the house up for sale. We packed precious memories to take with us—you know—photos, special cards and the like. We'd even packed junk— souvenirs— that we bought somewhere. What a sad—sad thing to watch the only person you ever loved so not remember much of anything any longer. There'd be times when she was afraid of me... She did not know who I was.

So—into the home we went—along with lots of other old people who had been put "out to pasture"... not worth much to people any longer. All of 'em hanging on in that home. Wheel chairs stacked up in the hallway. and waiting... just waiting to die. I had joined the stacks and stacks of wheelchairs of oldsters lining the hallways of the home. There they sat and vegged each day rarely noticing anything or anyone. Had a massive stroke and had to leave my Mary. 2 years later, she joined me here.(He pats her space) Guess dying is just part of life. We live... we die.

8—Terry Taylor. Age 32. I was the rich kid. The class beauty. People envied me because I was always laughing and seemed so happy. A cheerleader—did very well in all my classes... I never wanted for anything and I was popular.

After high school, I went to the best college that money could buy-Bryn Mawr—graduated. Married. God—I had it all.

Nobody ever knew that my dad abused me—sexually. From the age of 5, he visited my bedroom until I was 17. I told no one. He said no one would ever believe me and I was special. I was "Daddy's special girl". It was our secret! Who would ever believe me? He was a well-respected lawyer in town. We had the perfect family. It was in 1950... my husband, Jeff—kept saying that I seemed different. I grew cold and into myself. I refused his advances... refused to go places. He wanted me to get some counseling. I did alright. The first few sessions were ok... I opened up a little. Then he wanted to put me on a new anti-depressant medicine. Ludiomel. It was new on the market at that time and for a while I WAS feeling better about myself—the depression wasn't too bad. Then Jeff and I had a terrible argument... he blamed me for the failed marriage... our failed marriage. He rushed out the door... I couldn't think—I just raced around the house... trying to find what to do. where to go... In the back of my mind I always thought of suicide. And I even thought of how it would happen. Very stoic... Socrates like... I filled the bathtub with hot water—I sat in the tub. I took the razor – Jeff always used a safety razor... and carefully drew a deep line in each wrist. Then I laid back in the warm water and as the blood oozed; I fell asleep. At a 5 year class reunion, I know that I was the talk of the party once again. The rumors buzzed all "How could she do that? She had everything." My therapist was the only one I ever told. This is a secret I brought with me to the grave.

9—John Samuel Lane—55. Guess I lived a fairly normal life – whatever "normal" is... I voted. I went to church. I volunteered for community groups... A darned pleasant life with very special people... MY

FAMILY!. Ya know, if I could change anything about this "art of dying" it would be to legalize assisted suicide. When the cancer came back –the final time-stage 4 and vicious—My son, daughter and my wife and I had a sit down to discuss my final wishes. In most states assisted suicide is not legal... the poor schlep must just wait it out. Dr. Kervorkian made me sit up and notice when he carried out his mercy-killings. He respected the dying person by honoring their wishes... and not prolong their death. At the time only Oregon, Washington and Montana allowed assisted suicide. Is THAT person being kept alive... no just breathing... and for whom?... When/once the pain grew unbearable... absolutely agonizing, my wife asked the doctor to issue morphine patches... He did. In my mind, it STILL took an agonizingly long time for me to pass away. But my family was there every moment... they say that hearing is the last to go... it was. I could hear them telling stories, laughing some, crying some... playing music that I LOVED... The morphine was increased... and I was able to finally go in peace... day 4. If I was able to smile—I certainly would have been smiling on my own when I breathed my last. Against the law to allow someone to die with dignity??? Only my family knows.

10—I'm 16... well... almost 17!. The day I died was an ordinary school day. I wish I had taken the bus to school that day.

But I wheedled the car out of my mom saying "Special favor! All the kids drive once they get their license!" The final bell rang and I threw my books in the back seat. Freedom!... till 8:40 tomorrow! I was so excited—driving the car and being FREE! Oh—my name is Donald Ryan. It doesn't matter how the accident happened. I was goofing off... truth... I was texting my friend. I know I was driving a little fast. I was enjoying my freedom—showing off for my friends... I was having fun! The last thing I member I was passing this old lady who was going too slow. I remember a jolt and a crash! Glass and steel flew everywhere. My whole body was turning inside out. I heard myself scream... Then... nothing. Good old Barney Feiff—the village cop was standing over me. My body was mangled—I was covered in blood. Pieces of jagged glass were sticking out all over me. Strange – I couldn't feel a thing. Later I was placed in a drawer at the morgue and my mom and dad had to come to identify me. Why did my mom have to see me like this? Why did dad suddenly look like an old man? He told the man in charge, "Yes. That's my son."... The funeral was weird. One by one they passed by me and looked at me with the saddest eyes. Some of the guys were even crying.

A few of the girls touched my hand as they walked by.—they were sobbing. My brother and sister walked like zombies.

No one could believe I was dead. They buried me... me!! They each tossed flowers on my casket before they lowered me down. O please God—Hey—I've got a date tonight. I'm supposed to be going to college this fall. Give me just one more chance. Just one more (voice fades off)

11—Samuel or Elvira Altman. Died at age 87. It's a terrible thing to grow old... alone! Our kids got together and settled on a nursing home for Owen and me. It was attached to a hospital so they thought they were doing a kind thing for us. The day after we all sat in the living room of our home to discuss OUR immediate future, my daughter and her husband drove us to Pennsylvania to move in the old folks home. I had never thought that we would ever leave our home of 45 years. That was our home. Our whole life was there. The house was for sale that week. We never thought we would grow old! We were fooling ourselves... we aged. Samuel was nearly blind and somehow while trying to care for him, I fell down... often. I suppose it was time. Driving became impossible for me; the insurance company would no longer insure me. I realized that I should not be driving when I caused a terrible accident. I hated to rely on my grown children for rides... to the grocery, to doctor's appointments and the like. At least we were allowed to live together in the nursing home. But what an ugly experience-maybe it was a good thing that Sam couldn't see and I would be able to tend to his needs. After all—after 45 years of marriage—there were no secrets! The "home" was darned ugly-daily "residents" would be helped by aides to freshen up and then they spent the day in wheelchairs stacked up along the hallways. The ugly fluorescent lights made everyone look gray and... dead. Over-worked nurses and aides would speak to us as if we were babies. Most old ones never answered anyway. It's a pathetic thing to see a loved one—who can no longer see or hear, or taste... or remember. Sam sometimes knew me – most of the time... not. I held his hand as he passed away that cold January night – on My birthday! I wanted to go too. Afterward, My son would visit when he could and hold my hand... the hands that held him so tight when he was young. And now he held my hands with the transparent skin. Hands so frail and thin that he was afraid he would hurt me. "Gotta go now-mom," he said. I merely looked in his gorgeous blue eyes and nodded. That was the final time we spoke.

12—Name's Ernie... (hesitant). I don't do so well with speaking in p.p. public... forgive me... I always had a stutter. (composes self after a couple of deep breaths) –darn I REALLY worked on that! How I loved all sports! My nick-name was THE ELMIRA EXPRESS... #44! How I loved Elmira—The nabe... That is The neighborhood House where we played basketball, football... a great place for kids to hang out. I always thought that when I'd retire—I'd go back to the Nabe and work with kids... Most of the kids had lousy home lives... weren't doing too well in school – they... that is... WE all needed someone to believe in us! To steer us on a good path. I was a fortunate kid. I had all the right people in my corner... positive role models... and I was one of the lucky ones. I loved the whole city – my school... everything about Elmira, NY... most of all – I loved my faith. I tried – as hard as it was sometimes – to treat others as I wanted to be treated. Sometimes it was next to impossible... but there is nothing to be gained from hating back. My football career was just beginning and I was looking forward to playing pro ball with the Browns in 1961. I was so proud to receive the Heisman Trophy in 1961. Me. (modestly) little me... I graduated from SU with a degree in Business and made my mom so very proud. I LOVED LIFE!!! But in 1961 when I started to have frequent nose bleeds and my neck swelled... and I was just plain tired all the time—I ALWAYS. loved to eat but somehow my appetite just wasn't there... the doctors thought it was just mono-... Then the worst news ever—I was diagnosed with leukemia—Acute myleoid leukemia. In the 1960's, doctors did what they could and I was in remission for a while. Then... there was nothing more they could do. I passed away. peacefully... at the age of 23. Please love life while you have it... Oh. My name is Ernie Davis.

13—Nancy Britten—My epitaph! As BUSY housewife I FINALLY got to seep in!!! Me?. I'm nobody special. I am... I am just a housewife. Funny that word... like I was married to the house I always wanted to be the best mom I could be. My mom didnt work... oh— you know—she didn't have an outside job... outside of doing all the house chores. I wanted to be like her—be there when the kids came home for school, helping with the PTO, being a den mother for the scouts., being here when my husband needed me. I lived for many years as a contented housewife. Women's Libbers would get on my case. they'd suggest that I care more about ME. go to the gym, have an affair, drink, or join a book club... things like that. I did NONE of those things... nor did I watch day-time soaps. With 4 kids, 2 cats and our dog—I was ALWAYS busy. And then there was Jim—a devoted father and husband. It was IMPORTANT that he would come home to a. happy home... not just a house. Our home was spotless... Our children were respectful. Meals were always on the table at the right time... dependable time. Why—every Wednesday was our night for... making love. I don't believe I was ever bored or discontent. I was just ALWAYS busy. Well—maybe too busy to take care of my own health. Everyone else came first and I tried not to be a bother to anyone. I learned to be a martyr—mother... from MY mother. The day I died? Well—I was carrying a load of laundry downstairs and—somehow I tripped. I fell. I recall lying at the foot of the stairs... I couldn't move. The dog was looking at me. He nuzzled me to get up. I could not move—anything. I was paralyzed. At the hospital they told my family that had severe brain damage. I was in an "'irreversible coma". After a week, my husband signed the papers to have me taken off life supports. We had Never talked about death—or what would happen IF. or when... we were just going to have the kids grow up, leave and start their own families. And we would grow old together... just Jim and me... til "death do us part". I had no fancy dress to be buried in so Jim chose a skirt and sweater. I was always GOING to get myself a gorgeous dress for some special occasion... to feel pretty again. Someday! I said SOMEDAY alot. How sad that people live their lives around SOMEDAYS... someday I'm going to go here, someday I'm going to speak up... someday. wellyou know—we NEVER get another chance to live our one life. I would not build my life around somedays... I would act on these wishes... these dreams... hopes... plans. I would not defer them to a SOMEDAY.... Jim remarried 6 months after my funeral.

Oh. my name is Nancy Wright Britten.

14—John C. Allen here. I hope you can understand me alright— sometimes I get lock-jaw... jaw just freezes up. And that happened right after it. I was hit by a car while I was jogging. Never knew what happened it was all so fast! I understand that the young man was driving with a suspended license. Death was instant. I have no complaints about living—well—maybe except for the lady next door whose dog always barked during the night. Or maybe it was the sanitation guys laughing and making so much noise on Monday and Thursday mornings! Or playing golf in a pre-winter storm... and losing anyway. I had just become president of the company... I envisioned vacations in the Bahamas, sending my kids to prestigious colleges... most of all spending more time with my family and giving them a comfortable life!... a life of luxury! I had always thought to myself—when the time comes, I'll be ready. Well lemme tell you... you are NEVER ready! I read up on the after-life. Good ol' Sylvia Browne made me think about life "on the other side". And the Medium on TV—that whacky blonde with the spikey hairdoo... she got me thinking. The Long Island medium—that's the one! That's her name- I want to believe that somehow I can communicate with special people once this earthly journey is over. I rehearsed "walk into the light!!! What could it be like to "cross over?" and how would I do that! I never believed in the concept of hell or heaven—but I sure didn't want to go where it'd be hot always! In college, I remember reading Dante's "Inferno" and I told myself, "Never That! But then images of white fluffy clouds, and me prancing about in a white robe and... having a shit-eating grin on my face—forever—well that didn't seem so great either. Ok... so I've kept my secret of what it is REALLY like long enough. Ready? Ready for the truth? (clenches teeth) Oops. my jaw won't work... mumble mumble— (through his clenched teeth)—See you when you get here!

NARRATOR: We are all ON BORROWED TIME! What grave secret or secrets will you be taking to your grave? (lights gradually down to out... count of 6)

LINGER A WHILE

LINGER A WHILE a brief look at loving care in a retirement home by Someone Who Cares

SET: A modest "retirement home". Sign is posted of services offered "Short and Long Term care for the Elderly in a Loving Home". Modest living room. Center—there is a ramp leading to an opened double window that "supposedly" leads out onto the porch and lawn. However, the house is located on a cliff overlooking the sea and right below here is an abrupt cliff! This is where oldsters are dumped after being wheeled uphill in a wheelchair. A mattress or 2 are beneath the window for the oldster to land on once dumped. The furnishings are comfortable.

Stage left is a door leading to rooms for the seniors... all temporary rooms. DR is the front door wide enough for a wheelchair. It is a home for seniors to "linger... just a while."

CAST:

MARVIN is a greedy, lecherous and despicable cad with a calm tone of voice in the presence of "customers", fast, able to pull off a "sincere" demeanor that he cares but he is thoroughly rotten.

EDNA is a look-a-like for Peg Bundy. Stacked. A clothes whore. Overly made up. Loud. Giggly. Usually a cigarettes dangles from her overly red lips.

3 OLDSTERS (male or female) All are sweet and serene with wizened eyes and pitiable expressions. Possibly the same actor could pay "the old one" with wig, costume, knitting)

CINDY. 40ish, worn out

AT RISE: We hear the music being played, "Linger AWhile". Doorbell rings and we hear someone scampering away from the door outside. Marvin is at the top of the ramp as he has just taken care of an oldster. He wipes his hands and walks to the front door. He opens the door and reveals an Old One in a wheelchair. The oldster has just been dumped there.

MARVIN:

Well... well. well... what do we have here? (He deftly steers the wheelchair containing the oldster, 85, into the living room. The Old one sits holding a package of Depends in her/his lap.) Another foundling just dumped at our door. (Yells to Edna offstage left) Hey—honey. This one has a note pinned on her. (Marvin reads the note after ripping it off the old one as Edna enters with a cigarette dangling from her mouth.) "We can no longer afford to care for Aunt Martha/Uncle Ernest. Please help. You know what to do. (Edna wanders over to the mess stuffed into the wheelchair. The Old One sits staring)

EDNA:

And look—whoever dumped this old broad left us a package of Depends! Well, whoopy-de-do!

Now THOSE we can use... but her. NOT! (Laughs) SOoooooooooooo... (Marvin and Edna look at each other as they begin to rummage through the old one"s clothing looking for rings, etc. They do find a ring, 2 pennies and a dirty hanky. They "ooh" and "ah" once something is found. Marvin opens the Old One's mouth to find gold fillings but nada. The rifling is over and they look at each other. Marvin gestures to the ramp and window.)

MARVIN:

(As Edna is trying on her new valuables, Marvin pushes the wheelchair up the ramp.) There now—notice how the house butts right up against this steep cliff. Expedience!! (He dumps her off.)

He stands there watching her go and finally land. Then, he speaks as he slowly walks down the ramp.) This one didn't say a thing as she went down! Oh well—it's getting so that just anyone can just dump their old one on our doorstep!! Abandoning these poor oldsters like they were garbage! (He opens the front door and yells) Take care of your own trash! You hear me? (He closes door).

EDNA:

Now... dear... people know that we are a final resting place for their loved ones. They just don't know how "restful" is is here! (Laughs as she exits) And dear... don't forget to take out this week's trash! We sure barbequed her fast... nothing left now! The idea—loading her in here without any medicare etc. Just ashes! Nobody would know her now! (Holds up mail) Anyway—we still get Ethel's monthly checks... err... our monthly checks. Damned good thing her family never returned to see her. Knew they wouldn't! (She kisses the check.) Love you, Ethel!!!

MARVIN:

Near 25,000 bucks we made off that one! No one cared about her. Thank you, ETHEL. Love you, Ethel! (They both repeat and giggle. Doorbell rings. Marvin answers. There is a harried looking woman about 40 standing there with her VERY old one in the wheelchair. Cindy is well endowed with huge bosoms as is noted by Marvin.) You must be Cindy (as he oogles her breasts). It's good that you called. We just happen to have an opening here at "Linger A While".

CINDY:

Thanks so much for providing a good home for mom. She's a good old soul. (Hands over a small suitcase) I'm in a rush now... gotta get back to work... at Walmart! (She starts to go)

MARVIN:

Whoa there, sweety—you forgot something... the papers???

CINDY:

O, yes... mother's social security papers. I am signing over her allowance just as you suggested. She doesn't have many belonging anymore... my husband is selling the rest of them now. Craig's list! And Amazon. My husband wants to keep her antiques. Just some old photos left—worthless really—in her valise. Worthless to anyone.

MARVIN:

(Pre-occupied with rummaging and reading papers) Yeah—right... photographs. As much as we truly love all of our house guests, it IS necessary to keep up with costs of care. You understand.

(Looks over papers again.) It all seems to be in order... ah... yes... and now WE have the Power of Attorney! (Edna enters wearing apron as though she had been housecleaning.)

EDNA:

Well... look a here. This must be Jane. (She fusses over the old one.) We gunna take such good care of this one. Tell me—does she have any favorite foods?

CINDY:

She's fond of pizza but it needs to be pureed. You see, she has only a few teeth left now.

EDNA:

Don't you worry... we have our own way of making favorite foods liquidy. Good old blenders! And we have special little goodies for special little good girls. (She fusses over the lady, examines her gold teeth and finally speaks to the lady as if she were an infant and tweeks the old one on her cheek.)

MARVIN:

Do you plan to visit her anytime soon?

CINDY:

Oh—yeah... I'll have to call you on that. I have so much to do. Gotta clean out her room and fumigate. You know—she has lost control of her bowels too often—terrible smell. My husband-Ricky—is so demanding. He's a real sex maniac. Sex... sex... all the time! Honestly, I'm glad I go to work or he'd want it all the time I'm home. And my mom has been "in his way"—he says... thinks she is listening! And he bitches about her smell... after all it IS his castle! Now especially now that she's not there! (VERSION 2: one small kid is with Cindy. we see the kid kick the oldster, the helpless dog. "And I have 2 kids who need me... and 2 dogs and 2 cats.

The kids put up with her silliness somehow when she tries to tell them what her life was like... her childhood. But they could care less. We used to take her to church which she liked.

You know—the time and all that takes. She really is in the way. I just couldn't be bothered... errr. I mean... I just couldn't handle cleaning up after her and her messes any longer. It's easier with a family dog... an old dog. Just take him to the vet and he is put down. We really did try to give her a nice home since it is her house anyway (weak smile) We moved into her home... to make it easier on her. (She fakes tears and Martv and Edna try to feebly console her.)

EDNA:

O, we Love to clean up after them! After all—They can't help it! Don't you worry about thing. She is in good hands. We treat them as though they were our very own mom or dad. We LOVE (phony) them! Now—you run along and go to work hle we show mommsie around her new wee home.

CINDY:

Oh, thank you! Thank you! You are both such wonderful, caring people! I feel so much better now knowing that you will REALLY take care of her, (Edna gives her a tissue and Cindy honks into it.)

MARVIN:

Oh, we'll take care of her alright! (Edna and Marv smile knowingly at each other and then at Cindy. He opens the front door for Cindy) Here at LINGER AWHILE we care about our people! (as He shoves Cindy out, she weakly says "She loves bingo!!" and he slams the door fast.)

EDNA:

O, look! It's trying to say something! (The old one tries to say something but Edna takes her scarf and shoves in in her mouth to quiet her.) This one might actually come to visit her... really!

MARVIN:

Hmmm. I see her benefits don't kick in til the first of the month. OK then—granny. Looks like you'll have a room at least til then. You get to LINGER WITH US A WHILE! (he laughs.) Get it!... (He punches her arm but gets no response.) And, in case the state inspector comes around, we can show how well we take care of these old birds. That is until they reach their end! And, me lady, I might just diddle you a while, too!! (He starts to pull up the Old One's skirt)

EDNA:

O, you diddler, YOU! Such a sweet old lady! Such a sweet old lady! yeah—they check in but can only check out one way! (Marvin and Edna laugh and all 3 exit through the DL door. Once they exit, we see an OLD ONE carefully trying to navigate from the dorm area, DL door. He/She is encumbered by a cane and one leg that doesn't work too well. Eventually and painstakingly the Old One gets to the front door. Unrealized, he/she has tripped a wire at the front door announcing escape with a gaudy alarm! In rushes Marvin at top speed.)

OLD ONE (scared and angry)

I'm outta here! I'll go to the authorities and tell 'em what you're doin' in here! I gotta lots to say... I'm goin...

MARVIN:

Like hell you are! (He kicks the cane away from the Old One.) You've been a pain in the ass too long. Damn you! (He kicks and pummels the Old One as he/he is down. He concentrates on the stomach area to kick.) Your son gives us lots of money for us to put up with you, you smelly old thing. He's too busy with hs career... his family... his vacations to care about you any longer! You are in the way! So—we need to keep you alive... naw—keep existing. You ingrate... you scum bag.

We'll keep you here and that's what we WILL do. (Edna rushes in) Here, help me get this old fart back to bed. (They drag the Old One kicking and screaming back to the DL door.) You old dog... we'll fix you! (After they exit, Marv and Edna re-enter and arm in arm go up the ramp and look out the open window.) We've given so many their final rest! Rest in peace, Seniors!

EDNA:

Yes, and we have loved them all! (They begin to fondle while walking to the couch D C. Once there... they begin to fondle).

MARVIN:

Damn it, honey! We have to do something about that feisty one! She managed to give me a kick in the shin and it hurts, babe. That ungrateful... the price we pay for giving old ones such good care! All in good time... that one's days are numbered. A few more hunky checks and she's done! G... G... bye old one!! (They laugh.)

EDNA:

O my dearest... lemme kiss your boo boo! Mama make it all better! The good news is that we have 2 more ancient ones coming tomorrow and their fat government checks! (They laugh. They begin to ravage one another passionately. As the music, "Linger A While" swells OR they both sing, "So Linger A While!". End with Frozen smiles!)

Curtain.

61596227R00122

Made in the USA
Lexington, KY
15 March 2017